ONLY HALF OF ME

Rageh Omaar was born in Mogadishu, Somalia, in 1967. He began his career in the Africa Service of the BBC World Service, and from 2001 to 2003 he was the BBC TV News Africa correspondent, based in Johannesburg. He was BBC Television's main correspondent in Baghdad during the Iraq war and won an Emma award for the best TV journalist of the year from the London Press Club in 2004. Rageh Omaar is the author of *Revolution Day*. He lives in London with his wife and three children.

Only Half of Me

RAGEH OMAAR

PENGUIN BOOKS

PENGUIN BOOKS

Published by the Penguin Group
Penguin Books Ltd, 80 Strand, London WC2R ORL, England
Penguin Group (USA) Inc., 375 Hudson Street, New York, New York 10014, USA
Penguin Group (Canada), 90 Eglinton Avenue East, Suite 700, Toronto, Ontario, Canada M4P 2Y3
(a division of Pearson Penguin Canada Inc.)
Penguin Ireland, 25 St Stephen's Green, Dublin 2, Ireland (a division of Penguin Books Ltd)
Penguin Group (Australia), 250 Camberwell Road, Camberwell, Victoria 3124, Australia
(a division of Pearson Australia Group Pty Ltd)
Penguin Books India Pvt Ltd, 11 Community Centre, Panchsheel Park, New Delhi – 110 017, India
Penguin Group (NZ), 67 Apollo Drive, Rosedale, North Shore 0632, New Zealand
(a division of Pearson New Zealand Ltd)
Penguin Books (South Africa) (Pty) Ltd, 24 Sturdee Avenue,
Rosebank, Johannesburg 2196, South Africa

Penguin Books Ltd, Registered Offices: 80 Strand, London WC2R ORL, England

www.penguin.com

First published by Viking 2006
Published with additional material in Penguin Books 2007

1

Typeset in Monotype Bembo by Rowland Phototypesetting Ltd, Bury St Edmunds, Suffolk
Printed in England by Clays Ltd, St Ives plc

ISBN: 978-0-141-01715-0

For my parents,
Sahra Abdulkadir and Abdullahi Omaar

Contents

Prologue

Only half of me is the person you think I am. My first name is Rageh but this is only one of two names that I was given at birth. I was born in Somalia in 1967 in the first decade after independence from Britain and Italy, the two colonial powers who had divided the country into a northern protectorate governed by Britain, largely to safeguard its far more highly prized colonial possession of Aden, and the southern half ruled by Italy. Somalia, in the Horn of Africa, in the eastern Indian Ocean rim of the continent, joined the Arab League in 1974 and is an almost entirely Muslim country. The Somali language, whilst indigenous, is heavily influenced by Arabic and to a lesser extent

Persian and Hindi. At the time of independence Pan-Africanism, an intellectual movement that promoted the concept of unifying all continental black African cultures, was a strong influence on my parents' generation. The idea of Somalia as a newly independent black African nation was at the heart of the politics of the country, and to mark this my parents gave me the indigenous old Somali name of Rageh. Most Somali names have Arabic roots or have been taken from Islamic teachings. However, there is no Arabic equivalent for Rageh. It is pronounced with a hard 'g' as in 'gift' and no such letter appears in the Arabic language. When I travel through the Arab world I call myself 'Raajee' which is an Arabic name and means 'to hope for something good'.

My mother did not want me to have just a Somali name but an Islamic name too. There is a part of her that belongs to something else, an idea of who she and her family are which is not fulfilled by loyalty to a nation, however proud she is of it. She feels part of a much wider identity and culture.

In Islamic tradition God is said to have ninety-nine names. In the 'Hadith', one of the collections reciting the teachings and deeds of the Prophet Mohammed, based upon the memories and writings of the first converts to Islam who were 'the

companions of the Prophet', the Prophet Mohammed said, 'Truly, there are ninety-nine names of
God, one hundred minus one. He who enumerates
them will get into Paradise.' The first of the ninety-
nine names is Allah or God. The second is Abdel
Rahman which means the Compassionate. This is
the second name my mother chose for me.

When I telephone my mother in her family home
in northern Somalia, where she returned after living
in England for thirty-two years, she calls me Abdel
Rahman. Why did she give me that second name
and why is it so important to her? It is a question
that is a fundamental part of what it is to be Muslim
in the modern world – especially a Muslim living in
the West. Does your Muslim identity and loyalty
supersede loyalty to your nation? Do you feel
Muslim first and Somali, British, French or Dutch
second? Can the two identities really co-exist? My
second name also says something about the often
hidden aspect of Muslim lives in this post-September
11 world. Integration, at least as it is seen from the
perspective of Muslims coming to and living in the
West, is often about denying or even abandoning
half of ourselves. This book is a personal attempt to
show how that other half of us is an indivisible part
of our existence wherever we live.

★

It was June 1993, halfway through a complicated year. In May I had become a British citizen. Until that day I had felt like a foreigner. The deep Islamic green of my Somali passport now gave way to the burgundy of my new British one and as I put away that flimsy plastic booklet I realized, for the first time, that I was never going back. Each night as I watched the TV news in my London flat and saw the emaciated, nameless faces from a city at war and a country on the brink of destitution, I saw that the Somalia I had believed I would return to was disappearing. Britain, formerly a place of temporary exile, would now be my home and future. A new life.

Until the early 1990s I had not thought of a life in London. My parents had never believed we would stay. They had left Somalia before the catastrophes of war and famine had descended on our country and so had not come to Britain as exiles but to send us to English private schools to be educated in the skills that would help to build and renew post-colonial Somalia. It was temporary for them; it felt even more temporary for those who were forced to flee. I was at the tail end of the generation whose parents were convinced that their children would become part of a generation that would help lead Somalia towards the developed world. The civil war changed that.

I did not find it difficult in 1993 to cope with the idea of this different future. My family had already spent many years in Britain, I had had a privileged upbringing and education, and now, as a young man, I had the prospect of an exciting job. In the same year that I swapped my old passport for my new one my career prospects also changed. What had been a series of short-term contracts with the Africa Service of BBC World Service Radio was renewed as a longer-term contract.

However, the timing of my new job in my new country could not have been stranger. I spent every day in the office of Bush House in central London helping to produce the news on the very war and famine in Somalia that had ended the idea of my return there. The daily bulletins focused on the civilian casualties in Mogadishu as a result of the fighting between American forces and militia loyal to the main warlords, and the deaths of thousands more through hunger and disease.

I tried to help my colleagues in any way I could by speaking to Somali contacts, explaining the clan allegiances of various political and militia groups and talking to people from the BBC Somali Service and to members of my family, especially my sister, who was a prominent human rights activist whose writings on the war in Somalia were well known internationally. But it was not just the fact that this had been my country, or that I was reporting on the city where I was born that made the situation so unsettling. There was much more at stake. My mother's sister, Sophia, was living in Mogadishu; my father's only brother, Adan, also. We had many other close family friends and relatives in the city, all of them trying to survive in the midst of the horrifying events that I was editing, translating and analysing for the newsroom. We would receive reports from Mogadishu in the BBC office during the day and then, on rare occasions, a member of my family would get a barely audible telephone call at home as, down a crackling line, my uncle in Mogadishu would try to reassure us that everyone was safe. Some of my colleagues in the Africa Service knew my situation. They too had relatives in similar predicaments elsewhere: in Sierra Leone, Liberia and Angola. But most of my other colleagues and friends did not. What would I have told them? What could they say? It was a half of me that it was easier not to reveal. I felt too awkward, too out of place, so I never talked about it.

Then I was given my first foreign assignment as a journalist. I remember telling my parents that the BBC was sending me to report on Nigeria's first democratic elections after nine years of military rule.

Nigeria had been ruled by military governments for all but ten years since independence and so, unsurprisingly, the elections in 1992 held out particular hope for the Nigerian people. I remember the look on my father's face when I told him. He and my mother were thrilled, amazed that an institution such as the BBC would be sending an African to report on Africa. I had to bring us all slightly down to earth by reminding them that this was the World Service, not the distant summit of the BBC's domestic network news – but it did still feel like a triumph.

Lagos had lost its status as the capital of Nigeria in 1991, being replaced by Abuja in the centre of the country. Seeing Nigeria's former capital for the first time in June 1993 was overwhelming. I both loved the crowded, noisy city and dreaded it at the same time. It was black and West African and self-confident. The streets were jammed with orange buses shunting their way round the edge of the South Atlantic coast. To a Somali used to the emptier streets of 1970s Mogadishu and the balm of the Indian Ocean on the eastern rim of the continent, it felt very foreign.

Four days after I arrived in Lagos two British newspaper correspondents invited me for a drink at their hotel. When I got there I found the two middle-aged journalists drinking beer in the smoky bar. They greeted me warmly and we sat down and ordered more drinks. It was three weeks since I had become a British citizen and I was young, ambitious and eager to live up to the image of a foreign correspondent. The conversation turned to the conflict and famine in Somalia. 'Africa's big story of the moment,' as one of them described it. Both the journalists knew I was from Somalia; both had read my sister's reports on the conflict. I stiffened, preparing myself to present my views on the causes of the tragedy: where the roots of the civil war lay; whether it was the result of a Cold War indulgence of another African military dictator, or the failure to give an alternative framework for national politics and economic development outside of clan and familial allegiances. I waited for them to look at me.

They carried on talking. They continued to discuss the causes of the conflict, they compared notes on Mogadishu. I sat in silence, a spectator. One of them spoke of his recent assignment in the city and how he believed 'the clan system is really at the heart of this tragic mess'. Then, at last, he turned to me and, just as I was about to speak, he said, 'In fact, you know you ought to try for an assignment in Bosnia because there you'll just be seen as a Western reporter. If you try going to Mogadishu you'll find it much harder to report because you'll be seen as a Somali and everyone will want to know what clan you're from, and that could lead to problems for you.' I felt shocked and humiliated. I realized that no amount of privilege, education, knowledge or experience could shield me from moments like this, moments that would be familiar to every young immigrant, and which, since September 11 2001, would be particularly familiar to British Muslims: being silent while your identity is made by others.

Twelve years later, and it is August 2005. Just over half-way through another complicated year, one that was also full of grief and upheaval, but which offered hope too. In the weeks after the 7th July bombings in London the BBC held an internal seminar for the most senior executives from its different divisions. Investigative and crime reporters came to talk to the corporation's top management about the terrorist attacks and how they had been reported. Present at the seminar was a young, confident British Kashmiri woman, Saira Khan, who had recently come to national prominence in the BBC programme *The Apprentice*.

I had met Saira a year earlier, before her appearance on the reality TV show. It was five months after the fall of Baghdad and I had returned to live in Britain with my family. We rented a small cottage in west London and Saira and her English partner lived next door. We chatted, as neighbours who have much in common do. They told me about their wedding plans: how John was preparing to go through a Muslim ceremony, what he'd have to wear and what he'd have to say. A year later we had moved out to live nearby.

At the BBC seminar in August 2005 Saira spoke about what the BBC had meant to her as she was growing up in Britain. She described herself forcefully as 'mainstream Muslim' – the category within which the overwhelming number of Muslims of all ages would put themselves. Then one of the most senior investigative reporters in the corporation, Peter Taylor, intervened. He had just finished a series called *The New Al-Qaeda*. It was all very well, he said, to speak so optimistically about how 'mainstream Muslims' were now part of Britain's national life and institutions, but how would she explain to the BBC audience who sat listening to her so admiringly why some young Muslims had come to blow up innocent people and themselves on British trains? Without missing a beat Saira looked straight at Peter Taylor and said, 'Because those young Muslims are completely invisible to you.'

★

These two moments, twelve years apart, experienced by two different young British Muslims, one Kashmiri the other Somali, whose paths crossed briefly, reflect an experience that has intensified since London was bombed on 7th July. We, as a new generation of British Muslims, have to learn to speak about ourselves and our lives forcefully and honestly; to proclaim who we are. We need to explain how Islam as a living culture has changed from our parents' generation to ours. We have to describe our lives, not just to non-Muslims, but to ourselves as well and to our parents who do not know the extent to which our outlook is different from theirs and how our sense of identity is being radically reshaped by forces they did not experience. We have to describe our lives to those who know next to nothing about Islam and yet are hungry for an honest and authentic representation of our faith and culture today and want to understand where we feel it belongs in the British experience. And, perhaps, most important of all, we need to explain why the many voices in national public life, in the news media, arts, parliament, the police forces, legal system and think tanks, who talk of what is 'wrong with Islam' so proprietorially, should stop speaking on our behalf.

There are many fine and authoritative Western

academics, writers and journalists who have studied, explored and written about Muslim societies and have many acquaintances and friends from their experiences of these societies with whom to test their ideas and arguments. There are many other writers and journalists who, while not having the same level of expertise or experience, at the very least pose honest questions out of a genuine desire to be better informed about something which they don't understand and which frightens them. But neither of these two groups attracts the greatest attention or the most prominent platforms. That domain is still occupied by people who, until 7th July, were far removed from British Muslim life, not to say the existences of the poorer communities in Britain in general, both Muslim and non-Muslim, but who proclaim to know with certainty what lies at the heart of the 'Muslim problem'. How can this be? And how strange that they should know the answer when many Muslims are only now beginning to ask the right questions.

On 7 July 2005 four Muslim young men murdered fifty-two innocent people. Every Muslim feels they and their religion have been implicated. The search for answers and an understanding of how British society progresses from this tragedy has begun, and indeed must begin, with British Muslims asking themselves questions. What happened to these young men that made them do this? What failures contributed to turning them and their view of Islam towards much nihilistic violence? Why was it four *Muslims* who blew themselves up? Why have other marginalized communities not produced suicide bombers? What was it about their experiences at school, at home, in their communities, at work, among their peer group that changed them?

The call has been for a dialogue *within* Islam to try to find the answers to these questions. But there is no point in pretending that the responsibility rests only with British Muslims; that only when British Muslims sort themselves and their religion out will the violence and division in our midst be brought to an end. Where are the equally prominent calls for a dialogue *with* Islam and Muslims? The terrible events of 7th July have not only uncovered the existence of a range of problems at the heart of British Muslim society, but have also revealed the profound ignorance and fear of Islam that exists among many non-Muslim Britons. There are many Britons uncomfortable with the way British Muslims define themselves, and who see their religion as innately aggressive. Many Britons believe that Islamic political movements around the world are prone to the use of violence as an ideological tool, and there are very few mainstream voices in wider British society trying to challenge these stereotypes. Even since September 11 2001, most British people have been given little information about Islam or the Muslim communities of this country.

Before we begin to look at the communities themselves do we need to unravel the meaning of Islam? Who was the Prophet Mohammed? What did he preach and do in his life? What does the Quran actually teach? How can one analyse 'a crisis within Islam or the Islamic world' when reliable, expert knowledge of what Islam means is so glaringly absent from the mainstream media? Are Islam or British Muslims to be defined and represented to British society by the four bombers of 7th July? By Al Qaeda? Why are we surprised that Islam is often portrayed in stereotypical ways? Why is it seen by so many as a religion of violence and intolerance? Why presume that people in the West should be more aware of the true nature of our faith and identity? Why should British society accept that the roots of the violence committed in the name of Islam are to be found in politics and not the teachings of the Quran?

The ignorance about Islam should force British Muslims to confront preconceptions and orthodoxies of their own. I don't think we fully under-

stand the enormous cultural, historical and psycho-
logical distance that Western society has to travel in
order to refocus its perceptions about us. For 1,400
years Western civilization, as represented in its art
and literature, has depicted and defined Islam and
the Orient as alien, hostile and dangerous. 'Orientalism' is, as Edward Said's eponymous landmark
work argued, an integral feature of the Western
canon. The 'Orientalism' which Edward Said described in 1978 as the 'subtle and persistent Euro-
centric prejudice against Arabo-Islamic peoples and
their culture' would today be called 'Islamophobia'.
Whatever one chooses to call it, there is nothing
new about it.

Hundreds of thousands of British Muslims of
all generations, coming from nations as diverse as
Bangladesh and Nigeria, have been struggling for
two decades to redefine the relationship between
their faith and their new country – a struggle that
changes with every new generation. Millions of their
fellow Britons now want answers. Is there something
intrinsic about Islam that leads to violence? Is it the
idea of multicultural Britain that has failed? Is the
US evangelical Congressman who, in the wake of
September 11, described Islam as a 'violent and
barbaric faith' correct? What makes young British
Muslims from Pakistan, Eritrea and Somalia, who

have 'everything to live for', kill and be killed for the sake of Palestine, Iraq and Kashmir, countries they have never visited and conflicts they have never experienced? And why do they respond this way when their parents did not?

For the last forty-five years, since the first significant migrations from India and Pakistan, British society has seen and heard about Islam only through a series of snapshots in which much of the religion, culture and politics of Islam remained almost invisible. It has been in the gaps between those snapshots that the young Muslims 'blowing up trains' of whom Peter Taylor speaks were formed.

There are hundreds of thousands of people in the UK who hope and want to believe that 'I am Muslim and British' should not become a sentence that is ever harder to say; or at the very least that it should be a sentence that does not evoke a lingering sense of doubt in those non-Muslim fellow Britons who hear it.

I have spent the vast majority of my professional life so far reporting back to a British audience from the African and Islamic world. As a British Muslim in London after 7th July I did not recognize my life and the lives of my relatives in the representations I read in newspapers and saw on television. I don't see much that reflects the hopes and views of my nieces, uncles, cousins who have made their homes in Britain and elsewhere around the world. I hope that this book will bring to life the different voices and stories that I hear in my home and among my relatives and that, in doing so, it will offer a glimpse of an often hidden part of British society that is undergoing significant and vital change that will come to have a lasting impact on this country.

Since September 11 there have been documentaries purporting to dissect how 'Islamic terrorist cells' function and operate, there have been interviews with firebrand young Muslims shouting their violent intentions into television microphones. Documentaries have set out to explain the religion of Islam. We have seen examinations of concepts such as '*Jihad*' or what the Quran or the Hadiths say about 'martyrdom' or 'paradise'. These explanations have been linear, rational and empirical. Many of them have at their heart a desire to define the type of 'the Islamic terrorist' or 'Al Qaeda operative' and rely heavily on sociological, police and intelligence profiling which aims to uncover the 'mind of the suicide bomber' or 'global networks of Al Qaeda'.

Many Muslims who live in and belong to the same communities from which such men and women come do not themselves know the typology of suicide bombers. What they are able to describe are the varied, complex and constantly shifting identities and cultural forces that propel young men and women into interpreting politics through a violent religious prism. In the introduction to his excellent work *Al Qaeda: Casting a Shadow of Terror*, Jason Burke expressed it thus:

In the weeks immediately following the tragedy of September 11th there was a genuine interest in understanding 'why'. *Why* 'they' hate us, *why* 'they' were prepared to kill themselves, *why* such a thing could happen. That curiosity has dwindled and is being replaced by other questions: *how* did it happen, *how* many of 'them' are there, *how* many are there left to capture and kill?

This is not simply an appeal to people to be nicer to Muslims, or an attempt to prove 'what Islam has done for us', to proclaim Islam's contribution to Western civilization through its art, science and literature. Neither is it an appeal to people not to be prejudiced against Muslims because of their faith. Prejudice against and ignorance of Islam have existed for a millennium and a half and are not going to be overcome any time soon. However, what is different is that these caricatures are no longer a matter of prejudice, they are now a matter of life and death for *all* of us. The thread that runs through this book is the knowledge that what was first described as 'the War on Terror' has, sadly, become exactly that. Now, as in every war, you have to know who your enemies are, why they are your enemies and what you need to do to defeat them. The questions at the heart of this book that are uppermost in the minds of Muslims like myself are: do you know who among *us* are your allies? Are all of us suspect? If not, then who is on *our* side?

Only half of me is who you think I am. The image that you have been given of us British Muslims is only half of us.

1. Two Lives, Two Visions

I lived in a street just off the Edgware Road in north-west London from the age of five until I was twenty-five. When we first arrived, Edgware Road was a haven for wealthy Saudi and Kuwaiti families who came to London for their summer holidays, escaping the unbearable heat of the Gulf. A few years on and it had been transformed into London's 'Little Arabia', as thousands of less well-off immigrants from Middle Eastern countries settled in the area and began new lives in Britain. The first Iraqis I ever met were the Husseins, a family of Shias who opened a corner shop near our house in the mid-1980s.

As a child I would run into their shop on my way

home from school to buy sweets or I would be sent there by my mother for a pint of milk or packet of tea. Behind the till at the front of the establishment they had hung up a huge poster of an Islamic shrine which I didn't recognize at the time because I'd only ever seen pictures of the shrine at Mecca. I got to know the family well and one day I asked one of the brothers what the picture was and he told me it was a place called Karbala, the shrine of the son-in-law of the Prophet Mohammed, one of Iraq's holiest places.

The years during which my family and I lived along the Edgware Road witnessed some of the most important events to shape the Arab and Islamic world in the last hundred years. I grew from a young boy to a man during that time and became more politically aware and drawn to the events in the region of the world where my family's roots lay. The Russian occupation of Afghanistan at the end of 1979 had given rise to the creation of the Afghan *mujahideen*, funded principally by the United States and Saudi Arabia. It was a war in which young men from the Muslim world who wanted to go and fight against the Soviet forces were supported and aided in this effort by the Saudi Arabian and American governments and agencies, including Osama Bin Laden.

The Islamic Revolution in Iran – the defining moment in the birth of political Islam – had already taken place, in January of that year. A genuinely popular national revolution had overthrown a hated Western-backed secular monarchy, headed by the Shah of Iran, and installed a theocracy – the world's first modern revolutionary Islamic Republic. The Shah fled the country in January, and when Ayatollah Khomeini returned to Iran the following month from exile in France to head the revolution, over a million people came out on to the streets to welcome him back. Then, in neighbouring Iraq, a man called Saddam Hussein, who, I came to learn, was the president of the country from which the Hussein family originated, decided to invade the new Islamic Republic of Iran – and thus erupted what is without doubt the bloodiest conflict of the past thirty years.

Ayatollah Khomeini's statements, such as 'Islam is politics, or it is nothing at all,' would provide a new model for other Islamic figures and movements in countries also ruled by Western-supported governments.

Then, on 21 November 1979, an incident occurred which had an electrifying effect on people from the Arab and Islamic world: 250 young men entered the mosque in the holy sanctuary of Mecca. Ramadan had already ended and so the shrine was quite empty.

They were bearded and wore conservative Islamic robes and seemed pious and religious young men. But they had not come to pray. Within minutes, they secured parts of the shrine and declared that they had occupied the mosque in the name of Islam and Muslims, to seize it from what they saw as its corrupt defilement by the Saudi royal family. Violence in the shrine is absolutely forbidden, but there was no way the Saudi authorities could allow the situation to continue or negotiate with the young men, who had expressed their willingness to die, if necessary. Therefore senior clerics in the Kingdom passed a ruling stating that it was permitted in such an extraordinary situation to forcibly expel the militants.

The battle lasted several days as the young men fought through the vast tunnels, interconnected rooms and halls in the different levels of the sanctuary. The militants eventually reached the basement beneath the huge central courtyard of the shrine where they decided to fight to the death. To avoid bloody battle against men willing to die and which would undoubtedly lead to the death of many of the security forces, the Saudi authorities first tried to overcome the militants with tear gas. When this failed, the basement of Mecca's holy sanctuary was flooded. Then high-voltage cables were inserted into

the water and many of the young men were electro-
cuted to death. My parents remember how our
neighbourhood was obsessed with the news at that
time. Every Arab radio channel devoted hours to
the story. In conversations in the smoky cafés on
Edgware Road or with neighbours on our street
people could talk of little else.

By the time I was a young teenager the Iran–Iraq
conflict had dragged out into a long war of attrition.
Saddam Hussein had used chemical weapons sup-
plied by Western companies and the United States
provided his regime with the satellite pictures and
intelligence of Iranian forces he needed to maximize
the accuracy of his weapons and munitions. Then,
in 1982, came the disastrous Israeli invasion and
occupation of Lebanon and the siege of Beirut where
the PLO and its leadership were trapped by Israeli
forces. By the time I was taking my 'A' levels and
going into the Husseins' shop to buy cigarettes rather
than chewing gum, a Shia guerrilla movement had
been created to fight Israeli forces in southern
Lebanon. It was called Hezbollah. By this time
the neighbourhood around Edgware Road had an
unmistakably Arab feel to it. The Husseins' corner
shop was no longer the only one, and there were
many Arab and Muslim cafés and restaurants, travel
agents and halal butchers wedged between the older

---

supermarkets and pubs. On summer nights middle-aged men set down chairs outside their shops and chatted; the smell of water pipes, of roasting meat and spices mingled with the traffic and hung thick in the air.

When I left university I knew I wanted a life that would allow me to witness events in countries around the world which I felt were connected to my roots. I came back home to London and the Edgware Road, knowing that I wanted either to visit or live in the Arab and Islamic world, from which so many people in my neighbourhood had emerged. I spent June and July 1990 waiting for my degree results and writing job applications to newspapers, inquiring whether they might be seeking a keen though completely inexperienced young reporter to work for them in the Middle East or Africa. On 2 August, a bright, hot summer day in London, I got off the number 15 bus which stopped half-way down the Edgware Road, not far from Marble Arch. I saw large crowds outside two Middle Eastern banks further down the street; there must have been more than a hundred men and women there. People congregated on the street too: outside Ranoush, the Lebanese restaurant, and in front of one of the cafés where men usually sat quietly smoking Arabic water pipes. Something was wrong. The people seemed frantic. Several men clasped radios to their ears.

I walked back up the road towards our house. As I approached our front door, I saw my father with his arm wrapped around someone. It was our Kuwaiti neighbour, an old man who had been ill for some time. I had known him for years, he would always stop to speak to me when we met on the street and he would knock on our door on holy Muslim days and festivals to wish us well. I could see he was crying. My father saw me and gestured quietly for me to head on inside the house. I could hear my mother in the kitchen and I rushed in to tell her what I'd seen on my walk from the bus stop. She told me what had happened: 'Iraq has invaded Kuwait. Those poor people outside the bank, they must have been trying to get whatever they could of their savings. Is there no end to the upheavals in the Islamic world?' The repercussions from that event would change all our lives here in Britain and across the world.

As growing numbers of Arabs began to settle in Britain, the majority of them prosperous middle-class professionals, and many of them with the capital to be able to establish their own businesses, many newspapers and publishers started to spring up too. As so many governments in the Middle East were authoritarian and often frightening dictatorships, it made sense for news organizations and publishers to base themselves and their operations in Britain. With an ever expanding professional Arab population living in London and eager to work in a freer atmosphere, many of these organizations were run by people from the region they were broadcasting to and writing about. The explosion of London as a centre of Arab and Islamic media and publishing began at the time of the Gulf War.

The first major organization to base itself here was MBC, a free Arabic-language international news and entertainment channel with an estimated audience at the time of over 100 million. Many others have followed in the years since, including publications such as *Al-Quds Al-Arabi*, edited by the irrepressible and brave Palestinian journalist and writer Abdel Bari Atwan. In addition to these London-based publications, almost every Arab newspaper and news channel in the Middle East maintains a bureau in London. The city has become part of the story of the Arab Middle East: it is a major centre for Arab and Islamic writing, publishing and broadcasting and it is now one of the largest centres of political exile and refuge for dissidents from the Arab and Islamic world, whether they are secular politicians or radical clerics or just ordinary people who want to live their life in a way which they cannot back in their own countries. London is not simply a place where many Arabs live; it is a city where some of the most significant political and social discussion about developments in the Middle East are published and broadcast. This was the city I knew until I was twenty-five. This was home.

London has also become a haven for political exile and activism as well as writing and publishing for Muslims from South Asia, Iran and Africa, and is thus not just part of the story of the Arab Middle East, but also part of the story of Islam in the world. It has a vital role to play in the arguments that will shape how Islamic politics, society, identity, writing and art develop in the years and decades ahead. Paris, perhaps Berlin and Hamburg in Germany where 3 per cent of the population is Muslim, will be important in the context of Islam, as undoubtedly within the next decade will many American cities, given that Islam is the fastest-growing religion in the USA where there are more Muslims than in any other Western country, currently estimated at between 6 to 8 million. But no other Western city has anywhere near the importance that London has in the Islamic world. It led to French security and intelligence officials in the early 1990s labelling it 'Londonistan'.

In the eyes of French officials this was a pejorative term, a judgement on what the British capital had become with the apparently naïve and lax attitudes adopted by the British government and society towards Islamist political organizations and individuals who had been allowed to settle there and who were now advocating the overthrow of authoritarian regimes in the Middle East. Interestingly enough the first government to use the phrase in semi-official publications was Saudi Arabia, angered at the presence in London of Islamist opponents to the Saudi royal family. 'Londonistan' is a definition which deliberately sets out to undermine that part of London which connects the city to the Arab and Islamic world. 'Londonistan' sees London as a haven for militant violent Islamists. It is not about London being a home to some of the most important and influential Islamic scholars and learning centres in the world, such as the Al Khoei Foundation, established by the family of Grand Ayatollah Abdul Qassim Khoei, one of the most important Shia theologians of the last thirty years.

Nor is 'Londonistan' about the place which offered exile to the man elected to become Iraq's President in the country's first democratic elections,

Ibrahim al Ja'afari, aligned to the Shia Islamic list endorsed by Ayatollah Sistani. Mr Al Ja'afari, a medical doctor, joined the Islamic Al Da'wa party in Iraq at the end of the 1960s and fled Saddam Hussein's regime in 1980. He went first to Iran, but moved to Britain as a political refugee in 1989 where he became the London spokesman of Al Da'wa, preaching religious sermons during the month of Ramadan, and campaigning for the overthrow of the Saddam Hussein regime. As the President of Iraq after the much hailed elections of January 2005 he has been the Islamist most warmly received by President Bush, Prime Minister Blair and many other Western leaders.

'Londonistan' refers only to the radical young men from fringe organizations who hand out leaflets and sell videos about the conflicts in Bosnia or Chechnya, espousing an ideology of global conflict between Muslims and non-Muslims. 'Londonistan' is not about the London which is home to some of the most important news organizations and publications in the Arab and Islamic world, the London which is home to dozens of mosques, large and small, which raise funds for recognized Islamic charities working all over the world in areas of conflict and distress, including Kashmir, Palestine and Darfur, but also in places where there have been

natural disasters which have affected Muslims and
non–Muslims alike, such as the tsunami in South and
South-east Asia.

After the 7th July bombings in London, this label,
which had rarely been used by British commentators and newspapers before, suddenly became
ubiquitous. It formed the basis of reports by BBC
Television news' main bulletins. Left-wing and
right-wing publications from the *Daily Telegraph*
to the *New Statesman* printed anxious pieces about
'Londonistan'; even the *London Review of Books* was
not immune, publishing an article about being 'in
the streets of Londonistan'. Which streets? Streets
around Regent's Park? Or Queen's Park, home to
the mosque where Ayatollah Abdul Majid al Khoei
worshipped and where Yusuf Islam, formerly Cat
Stevens, has established a Muslim teaching academy
for young people? Or the Edgware Road where
I grew up?

My brother and his family still live off the Edgware
Road. It is the same flat, on the street opposite the
tube station, where I lived until I was a teenager,
before we moved to a house further down the road.
My brother's children, my teenage nephews and
niece, who were born in Britain, make the same
journey to school every day, on the tube from

Edgware Road station, which I did when I was a child. At 9.20 a.m. on the morning of 7 July 2005, I tried to board a District Line train at Turnham Green tube station in west London, but the station was closed due to 'a major power failure'. I caught an already packed bus, joining the millions of other Londoners affected by the shutdown of the city's transport system, the true cause of which none of us at that point knew. As the minutes passed and the crowds at each bus stop increased, many of us began to realize that something very unusual, very wrong was happening. One young man standing in the middle of the bus was listening to radio reports through his mobile phone. He shouted out to the other passengers the news that there had been an explosion on a bus in Tavistock Square, and that it also seemed certain that there had been a series of bomb attacks in London. One of the explosions, the young man said, had been at Edgware Road tube station.

The mobile phone system set up to give priority to emergency service calls and signals throughout the capital were collapsing. I was desperate to call my brother. The signal on my phone came back for a minute. My brother answered. The moment he spoke I scanned his voice for any sign of fear or panic, any suggestion that something catastrophic had happened. But he sounded his usual self. He hadn't heard the news, he hadn't heard an explosion. He'd seen the children off to school, but thankfully they had gone by bus that day. He had to go. He needed to call them immediately.

It was not clear then that the explosions had been caused by British Muslim suicide bombers, but it was clear that the people or organization that had carried out the attack, whether by remote device or otherwise, were almost certainly linked to the Al Qaeda network. The Prime Minister, who was attending the G8 summit of world leaders at Gleneagles, made it clear in his speech. The bombers, whoever they were – at that time we did not know they were four young British-born Muslims – had wanted to kill as many people as possible. The bombers could not have know what colour, faith, political opinion or sex their victims belonged to. However, they did know that they were carrying out their attacks in one of the most racially, religiously and culturally diverse cities in the world. They did so in the name of a global religion and culture: Islam. So, why did they choose to explode one of their bombs at Edgware Road tube station? Throughout that terrible day, as I, like millions of other Londoners, found out that there had been four bomb attacks by individuals linked to Al Qaeda, I found myself asking this question again and again.

Edgware Road is not a central station for commuters like King's Cross or Aldgate where thousands of people race through the turnstiles during the rush hour and where the terrorists could expect numerous casualties. If the perpetrators of the bombings had embarked on this course of action in the name of Muslims disenfranchised, impoverished and brutalized by conflicts in the strategic interests of Western powers, why would they bomb a station in the heart of the largest Arab Muslim district of London? Had our luck been any different that day, had my brother decided to visit colleagues in Whitechapel that morning and had he caught the train at Edgware, or had my aunt, my mother's closest sister, who was staying with my brother at the time, decided to visit relatives via the underground that day, or had my nephews and niece gone to school on the tube, or had friends of ours set off for work a little later, then ten members of my immediate family or their friends could have been killed that morning. All of them Muslims.

The bombers could not have failed to know what sort of community Edgware Road was. The heartland of British Muslim life was their target. It emerged later that the Edgware Road bomb was detonated by the leader of the four bombers,

Mohammed Sidique Khan, a thirty-year-old bright and successful teaching assistant from Beeston in Yorkshire, who was the father of a young girl and the husband of a British Pakistani woman who worked as a teacher. He played the pivotal role in leading the other three younger bombers. Why, as the ringleader, did he choose Edgware Road as the target for himself? Why not one of the other targets? Mohammed Sidique Khan, wearing the red and white *keffiyeh* which is the customary headscarf worn by men principally in Saudi Arabia, made a video recording justifying the bombings before they were carried out. Several months after his suicide attack, Mohammed Sidique Khan's words were broadcast on television. His speech was stilted and self-conscious as he blandly reiterated the dogma of the fight for 'my people' who were being 'tortured and gassed' around the world. But there was nothing revealing in the words he had recorded.

Mohammed Sidique Khan chose Edgware Road as a target, and selected himself as the leader of the bombers to detonate the device there, because it was a symbol of something that he and the movement he followed despised. They attacked Edgware Road precisely because it represented a relationship be-tween Islam and the West, a cultural and ideologi-cal abomination to those who believe in the pure interpretation of Al Qaeda's message. They were attacking the idea that Islam as a religion and Muslims as a community can thrive in the West – in London or Paris or Manchester or Hamburg. They were also attacking the idea that you can have a British identity but still be a part of the wider global 'nation of believers'. The belief that a western city can ever be a part of the modern story of Islam in the world is sacrilegious to the fundamentalist vision.

Edgware Road presents more of a challenge of legitimacy to Al Qaeda than a western society where Islam does not play an active and positive role because Al Qaeda is on the side of those who argue that multiculturalism has failed and should be abandoned. Their only response to their own frustration and the suffering of other Muslims around the world is revolution and vengeance, just as the only solution put forward by the West is to abandon religion altogether and firmly ally yourself with one nation. Few Muslims believe in the absurd idea that Al Qaeda is fighting on behalf of or in the name of Islam. More Muslims have died in the 'War on Terror' as a result of British and American policy on the one hand, and as a result of Al Qaeda's attacks on the other, than people of any other religion. Many, many more Muslims have been victims of terrorism since September 11.

★

On 21 July 2005 London was again subject to a city-wide emergency as four suspected suicide bombers tried and failed to carry out a number of explosions. The attacks were apparently a conscious imitation of the devastating series of bombs exactly two weeks earlier. Three of the bombers targeted underground stations while a fourth tried to explode a device on a bus. But, though the detonators exploded, the devices failed to go off. London's transport system was again brought to a halt. Connecting underground lines and stations were evacuated and some of the busiest roads and areas of London were emptied of all people and traffic. By the next day, a nationwide search was launched for the four suspected bombers, whose faces had been caught by closed-circuit television cameras.

Four days after the failed attacks came the news that brought fear to every Somali in Britain. Police identified one of the bombers, Yassin Hassan Omar, as a Somali now permanently living and settled in Britain. Whereas three of the four suicide bombers of 7th July were second-generation Britons from well-established Pakistani immigrant communities, the 21st July bombers were all child immigrants who had arrived in Britain ten years earlier, fleeing wars in the Horn of Africa. Their terrifying journey from conflict in their home country to a life in Britain was shared by hundreds of Somali families and children. Then the second of the suspects, Osman Hussein, a naturalized British citizen, was also originally identified as being from Somalia (though he was actually from Ethiopia). Within days of this information being released, articles and television news programmes set out to try to understand the Somali community in Britain.

Most of the accounts in British newspapers of Yassin Hassan Omar's life said he grew up in Somalia. In fact he grew up in eastern Ethiopia, in the overwhelmingly Somali region of the country known as the Ogaden, named after the semi-arid desert between Ethiopia and Somalia which has formed the natural frontier between the two countries for centuries. He grew up in the frontier town of Harar, an ancient walled city sitting on a hilltop and from where you can look out on the last vestiges of the still verdant highlands of Ethiopia, before descending to the largely nomadic and parched dry lowland Somali plains. The journey from Yassin Hassan Omar's home town, Harar, to my own family's home town of Hargeisa in northern Somalia is no more than 136 miles, although given the state of the roads it would take practically half a day to cover that distance. In 1992 I travelled from London to

Harar and then on to Hargeisa. That same year Yassin, then aged eleven, made the same journey but in the opposite direction, from Harar to London, a young refugee boy escaping the war that had engulfed Somalia and was soon to plunge the south of the country into an appalling famine.

Harar grew from the seventh century onwards as a result of the trade routes established by Arab settlers along the present-day Somali coast which ran between the Arabian Peninsula and the hinterland of modern-day Ethiopia. Because of this early Arab and Islamic influence, Harar developed not simply as an important trading post, but also as a centre of Islamic culture and religion in the Horn of Africa. To this day there are nearly a hundred mosques within the relatively small confines of the old walled city. It was in this city renowned for religious learning that Yassin Hassan Omar grew up. Like all boys his age and from his background he would almost certainly have attended a Quranic school or *madrassa* from primary school age. There would have been no other source of education in the town. The civil war in the north of Somalia, which ended in 1990 with the declaration of independence by the unrecognized Republic of Somaliland, left the region in ruins. Harar, like so many other towns in the area, descended into lawlessness and the region became the centre of one of the world's biggest international refugee crises.

In 1992 Yassin finally left the country with his sister and her husband and they settled in north London. For them, as for thousands of others of the same background arriving in Britain at the end of the 1980s and beginning of the 1990s, the transition was very difficult. They had witnessed a civil war, passed through vast refugee camps and suddenly arrived in the United Kingdom, having up until then known little about the world outside Ethiopia and Somalia. Yassin was one of those who could not adapt. The following year, at the age of twelve, he was taken into care. He was not placed with another Somali family or with Africans or Muslims but with a Christian Afro-Caribbean family. This move marked the beginning of a relentless cycle of different foster families and care homes. He would live like this for six years.

When he was eighteen, Yassin was given 'exceptional leave to remain' in the United Kingdom but was rightly deemed by social services to be 'a vulnerable young adult'. By then Yassin Hassan Omar must have had no idea who he was. He had long lost all contact with his Somali past, its culture and, most importantly, his family. He must have remembered his childhood in Harar, a world that had nothing to do with his experience in foster homes during the critical and confusing years of growing up. Which part of him was British? Or Somali? Or Christian? Or Afro-Caribbean? He was provided with a one-bedroom flat in an estate in north London, paid for by the local council. It was during this period that he met and befriended a young man who often came to stay with him at his flat. His name was Ibrahim Muktar Said, and he would become the ringleader of the 21st July bombers.

Like Yassin, Ibrahim arrived in Britain in 1992 – the same year as Yassin – as a child refugee from conflict and displacement in the Horn of Africa. He was fourteen years old. His family claimed asylum as refugees having escaped another war, in Eritrea, which had been fighting a three-decade-long war of independence from Ethiopia. Ibrahim also failed to adapt, but he was not as nervous as Yassin and was, at least superficially, much tougher. He began smoking cannabis and at school he gained a reputation as a bully. When he was sixteen he ran away from home, having become estranged from his family, and joined various youth gangs. In 1996 he was jailed for five years for violent robbery and was sent to several young offenders' institutions. One of them was Feltham. It was a critical moment, because it was at Feltham that he was converted to a radical vision of Islam. It was similar to the experience of Richard Reid, the so-called 'shoe bomber', who also attended Feltham Young Offenders' Institution. In this isolated environment Yassin became a devout Muslim. To this day, Somalis constitute one of the largest minority groups in Feltham.

These stories are not intended to argue that social deprivation or alienation are somehow solely to blame for terrorist acts by young British citizens and residents like Yassin Hassan Omar. Failing to adapt, isolation from family and home, exposure to older and intimidating people from a similar background are only some of the factors that lead a young man to commit horrific crimes. There are hundreds of thousands of other child refugees – from Somalia, Afghanistan, Iraq and many other countries in South Asia, the Middle East and Africa – who have endured the same experiences, but have not headed in the same direction, just as there are thousands of white teenagers from foster homes who do not end up in young offenders' institutions or become violent criminals.

As you read these pages, many more child refugees from conflicts and repressive regimes in Muslim countries will be arriving in Britain. Is Yassin Hassan Omar representative of what they will become in Britain? Which questions we ask is what defines our joint response to this crisis: do we ask what happened to these particular young men, or do we ask what's wrong with the faith and community they belong to and in whose name they acted? It is because so many more people ask the latter question rather than the former that Somalis in Britain and the Muslim community in general feel so powerless. They do not wish to defend their faith in this context because to do so would be in some way to acknowledge that it is religion that drives these young men to act as they do.

The figure of Yassin Hassan Omar is held up as an example of how his religion cannot work in the modern world. The idea that this individual, or indeed any individual, could be representative of an entire religion seems absurd in any context, let alone when you consider his life story. At the same time, another individual is held up to us as representative – in this case as an apparently positive example of how Muslim immigrants can adapt to 'modern' values. It is presented as the correct and progressive antithesis to Yassin Hassan Omar's story.

It was a bitingly cold November day and the entrance to London's Institute of Contemporary Arts was filled with people savouring the rush of warm air in the small atrium as they took off their gloves and heavy overcoats. It was a late midweek morning, and so the audience was modest at first. But soon the numbers began to swell with a different sort of crowd. Journalists and national television crews milled around the entrance. Anxious-looking press officers rushed about informing everybody that the event was a little delayed because 'the special guest' had only recently landed at Heathrow and was stuck in traffic on the M4 into London. I saw two friends from *Channel 4 News*: a young and talented South African television producer with whom I'd worked when he was at the BBC, and one of Channel 4's main presenters, who was also a British Muslim. The three of us chatted, wondering why we and several other representatives of the national media had been sent to cover what all of us agreed was, by any standard of news programming, a non-story. Soon another journalist arrived, a writer from the *Sunday Times*, closely followed by two PR people from a leading British publishing company.

We had come to attend a literary event starring a young Somali-born woman, Ayaan Hersi Ali, who was now a member of the Dutch Parliament. Hersi Ali's father, like mine, was an opponent of the Siad Barre regime and had had to flee the country. The family was forced into the peripatetic existence of all political exiles – constantly on the move as the regime exerted political pressure or concluded deals with other countries in order to make it difficult for its opponents to settle there. She and her family lived in Saudi Arabia, then Ethiopia, before finally settling in Kenya, where Ayaan attended secondary school. Her upbringing throughout these years was a strict Islamic one. The young Ayaan Hersi Ali was a stern, devout young Muslim girl who wore a full *hejab* and studied the Quran. Her life was to change suddenly and permanently when her father decided on an arranged marriage for Ayaan with a cousin in Canada. The papers to get her into Canada were to be processed by a relative living in Germany. Ayaan travelled to Germany, to spend a few nights there before her onward voyage to Canada and the life arranged for her. But in that time something inside her, a voice or a sudden discovery of inner strength, told her not to go through with it, and she escaped. She would have to abandon everything: the arranged marriage, her family, her relationship with them and her home.

She took a train to the Netherlands, where she claimed asylum as a Somali single woman escaping the ravages of the war in her country. The only way she could hope to gain admission was to omit the details of her family's residence in Saudi Arabia, Ethiopia and Kenya and to claim to the Dutch authorities that she had arrived directly from the violence and chaos of Somalia. Like many other Somalis faced with the similar prospect of not being able to return to anywhere they could call home, but whose circumstances did not fall within the exact legal requirements for gaining immediate political asylum, she understandably omitted the details which stood in the way of gaining entry into the West. As a result she was given A-status refugee asylum and permitted to stay indefinitely in the Netherlands. She was without any family, and began a new life.

Cut off entirely from the people and world she knew in a country where she had no connections, Ayaan Hersi Ali began to remake herself. Like Yassin Hassan Omar, she was now in a terrifyingly different world. She was sent to an asylum seekers' centre in Leintern, where she was given a series of menial jobs and where she helped to translate for other recently arrived Somali immigrants. She progressed through the well-meaning yet deadening bureaucracy of the Dutch refugee and asylum system. Her aim was to gain a university education, and after being directed to a series of clerical jobs which merely prolonged her dependence on the state, Ayaan finally managed to attain her goal in 1995 when she was able to enrol at Leiden University to study political science.

It is at this stage that her voice begins to show the

first signs of the zealotry of a new convert, rejecting a set of beliefs which has previously defined their identity, and embracing everything to which those beliefs seem diametrically opposed. Ten years after she enrolled at Leiden University, and only a few months before I began to try to get an interview with her, she spoke of how the experience changed her, and forged the set of beliefs for which she is now globally celebrated in liberal circles. She took the degree, she said in an interview to the *Guardian* on 17 May 2005 under the title 'Danger Woman', because 'I wanted to understand why all we asylum seekers were coming here, and why everything worked in this country, and why you could walk undisturbed through the streets at night, and why there was no corruption, and why on the other side of the world there was so much corruption and so much conflict.'

Ayaan readily admits now that her initial vision was rose-tinted but her early statements reveal a young eagerness to embrace a Utopian dream. 'Imagine! Everybody is reasonable. Everybody is tolerant. Everybody is happy. Your biggest worries are: will I get my grades? And do I have a boy-friend? And did I party well last night? And then, you have vacations!' The flip side of this conversion to a new western Utopia was an absolute and insistent rejection of her past. It was not a simple matter of no longer wearing a headscarf or avoiding alcohol, not praying or fasting. There are millions of people who regard themselves as Muslims belonging to Muslim families and a Muslim culture who drink and don't fast. By her own admission Ayaan wanted to get away from everything that reminded her of what she had left behind.

After leaving university she worked as a researcher for left-wing think tanks. She was assigned to a policy unit concerned with immigration and asylum. Since the 1960s, with an ageing population which would be unable to sustain the country's continued economic and industrial growth, the Netherlands had encouraged and admitted large influxes of migrants, many of them from Muslim countries such as Morocco and Turkey. The wave of immigrants was the means to satisfy the country's need for labour across the national economy. The state system for the settlement of migrants was built around a policy of integrating them into Dutch society, while also respecting and enabling communities to maintain their religious and cultural identities. As a result Muslim communities were allowed to have their own schools, mosques and social and cultural organizations. It had been this way since the seventeenth century when Catholic, Protestant and Jewish schools and institutes were set up for their own communities.

This was exactly the period when the controversial and populist extreme-right-wing politician Pim Fortuyn had become very popular in the Netherlands and had begun to outstrip the Labour Party. He courted popularity and attention by promoting a hatred of Islam and immigrants. He was quoted in August 2001 in the *Rotterdams Dagblad* as having said, 'I am in favour of a cold war with Islam. I see Islam as an extraordinary threat, as a hostile religion.' His policy was to severely restrict all immigration to the Netherlands but, in particular, if he came to power, he would stop all Muslim immigration. He declared that 'If it were legally possible, I'd say no more Muslims will get in here.' He was asked by the national *Volkskrant* newspaper whether he hated Islam. He replied, 'I don't hate Islam. I consider it a backward culture.'

It was a new political climate which chimed with the social and philosophical trajectory which Ayaan Hersi Ali was embarked on. She produced the findings from her research for the Labour Party and recommended that the policy of allowing migrants, but particularly Muslim migrants, separate schools and cultural institutions be dismantled. Her reports proposed a policy of shutting down the Netherlands' forty-one Islamic schools and strongly curtailing the levels of immigration.

Then inevitably Ayaan began writing numerous articles and tracts which echoed the views and comments of Pim Fortuyn; virulent attacks and denigration of Islam as a faith and as a culture which she argued was incapable of integrating into Western liberal society. She also condemned specific social practices in a number of Muslim countries which had already rightly been condemned by many other Muslim men and women for decades, such as female genital mutilation and oppressive laws and customs against women. But much of the broad thrust of her writing and criticism of Islam was as a culture and identity that simply did not and could not fit in with Western values, which to her were intrinsically more advanced, more 'civilized' and less 'barbaric'. Her attacks on Islam as a religion and as an identity are not related to specific issues – be it Islam's role in multiculturalism, or women's rights within Islamic societies or even the general issue of immigration. After all there are many European Muslim writers, academics, novelists, journalists, politicians and activists who have been critical of and spoken out on all these issues for a long time. The vital difference is that Ayaan Hersi Ali's criticisms of and objections about Islam are so absolute. It is Islam and how it is practised by Muslims which are the problem, full stop. The idea that arranged marriages are as much a part of Hindu tradition as they are Muslim, that genital mutilation is common practice in non-Muslim African villages, or that oppressive laws against women are enshrined by avowedly secular governments were not part of Ayaan Hersi Ali's debate.

Ayaan Hersi Ali broke with the left-wing Labour Party and was wooed to the right-wing VVD party, who adopted her as a parliamentary candidate on its list. Her comments became ever more vitriolic. On 25 July 2003 she gave an interview to the national newspaper *Trouw* in which she said of Prophet Mohammed: 'measured by our western standards, he is a pervert. A tyrant', and that the Prophet had 'tried to imprison common sense'. It was at this stage that she began to receive death threats by fanatics who rather than argue with her and take issue with the bigotry and hate with which her arguments were allied, wanted to silence her by killing her. She was given immediate protection by the Dutch authorities and was accompanied by bodyguards wherever she went.

Ayaan's next project was with the maverick film-maker Theo Van Gogh, who admitted that the aim of his films was to provoke and disturb. In interviews he described Muslims as 'goat fuckers'. His comments were more extreme than those of Pim Fortuyn and Ayaan Hersi Ali, both of whom he admired and said he supported as politicians. In 2002, to widespread horror in the Netherlands and the rest of Europe, Pim Fortuyn was assassinated by a man called Volkert van der Graaf, an agriculture graduate who said he feared that Fortuyn posed a threat to 'vulnerable members of society'. Ayaan Hersi Ali was Fortuyn's political heir, and after his murder she continued to espouse the same arguments about immigration and Muslims which he had put forward. Theo Van Gogh lent her his full support.

In 2004, Theo Van Gogh and Ayaan Hersi Ali decided to collaborate on a short film called *Submission*, in which they wanted to portray what they saw as Islam's inherent brutality and casual sexual violence and which they believed were an integral part of the teachings of the religion and culture. The script, written by Ayaan Hersi Ali, spoke of how husbands beat and punched their wives regularly but how despite this the women were prepared to submit to Allah's will as Islam proscribes. Verses from the Quran were painted on naked and abused female bodies. Muslim organizations and national bodies complained that this was an inaccurate representation of the teachings of Islam. On 2 November, as he cycled along a street in Amsterdam, Theo Van Gogh was shot dead by a young Muslim, who then slit Van Gogh's throat and, with another knife, pinned a note to his body by stabbing him in the torso.

Ayaan Hersi Ali fulfilled her commitment to Theo Van Gogh before his brutal and senseless murder by making a sequel to the film *Submission*. It was shown at the ICA in London on the evening of her talk at the institute.

In the twenty-four hours she was in London and during which I tried to see her for an interview, Ayaan Hersi Ali was interviewed by the most prominent and high-profile radio and television programmes and publications in the United Kingdom. She started the morning with a long interview on BBC Radio 4's *Woman's Hour*, she was then interviewed by *BBC News 24*, followed by her appearance at the ICA during which she was interviewed by Helena Kennedy QC, who had taken time off work specially. A news crew for *Channel 4 News* were there to record a report about her ICA recital and press conference which was to be run ahead of an interview by Channel 4's anchor Jon Snow. She also spoke to the *Sunday Times*.

It was the kind of attention that most politicians

and prominent artists dream about. And yet Ayaan Hersi Ali had not come to make a new political statement or launch a new campaign. Her appearances were to publicize a book consisting of a collection of articles on free speech of which she was one contributor. As we went into the lecture hall of the ICA my friend the producer from *Channel 4 News* talked wearily of 'the kind of liberal fascism' which lionized Ayaan Hersi Ali, but which was seemingly unwilling to think about what he described as her 'open flirtation with bigotry and hate speech'. 'Having grown up as a white South African whose family are members of the ANC,' he said, 'it's hard to make out the difference between what she says about Muslims and what Eugene Terreblanche [the Neo-Nazi Afrikaans politician] said about black South Africans.' Once we were all inside and the security guards had taken up their positions outside the doors to the auditorium, Ayaan Hersi Ali made her entrance, walking up to the stage where she was greeted by Helena Kennedy. A fellow writer and editor of the book of collected essays paid a brief but fulsome tribute to Ayaan, describing her as 'the incarnation of everything freedom of speech is about'.

In 2004 Ayaan Hersi Ali was awarded one of Europe's most prestigious prizes, the Prize of

Liberty, by Nova Civitas, a liberal think tank. At the end of that year she was awarded the Freedom Prize by Denmark's Liberal Party, which was presented to her by the Danish Prime Minister Anders Fogh Rasmussen. The following year another Liberal Party, this time in Sweden, awarded her the Democracy Prize. Then, amazingly, *Time* Magazine named her one of the 100 most influential people on earth. She was featured in the 'Leaders and Revolutionaries' section of the world's most influential people. According to *Time* Magazine, Ayaan Hersi Ali belonged alongside, among others, Hu Jintao, the President of China; Mahmohan Singh, the Prime Minister of India; Cardinal Ratzinger, now Pope Benedict XVI; President George W. Bush; former President Bill Clinton; Gordon Brown, the Chancellor of the Exchequer; Thabo Mbeki, the President of South Africa; Condoleeza Rice; Donald Rumsfeld and Ariel Sharon. *Time* Magazine included only three other Muslims on the list: one was Mahmoud Abbas, the President of the Palestinian Authority; the other two were Grand Ayatollah Ali al Sistani, the spiritual leader of Iraq's Shia community, and Abu Mousab al Zarqawi, the leader of Al Qaeda in Iraq. *Readers' Digest* selected Ayaan Hersi Ali as European of the Year for 2006.

The right to free speech is unquestionable, the

horror of Theo Van Gogh's murder and the heinous views of his killer are beyond any doubt. But these two points do not explain why Ayaan Hersi Ali's views are treated with such reverence. There are many other writers who, like her, campaign vociferously for freedom of speech, many of them Muslim women. They receive little or no attention. What explains such adulation and veneration? What is it about her that puts her so beyond reproach, her arguments and the repercussions of her views so beyond scrutiny? Have those newspapers who carried profiles of Ayaan Hersi Ali looked into the effect her speeches have had on the public view of Islam, not to mention in the literature of European Neo-Nazi underground groups who believe in an eternal war between Christian and Muslim civilizations? Ayaan Hersi Ali's official website carries a contribution from a man who calls himself Antonio G. It reads as follows:

Are you a male who harbours secret rape fantasies and impulses? Islam gives you the right to rape (in your opinion) indecently dressed women or to take 'temporary wives' in combat. Are you a secret barbarian who does not want to work and would prefer to participate in barbarian raids on hard-working productive citizens of other cultures? Your marriage unsatisfying to you and you want an easy divorce? Want to vent your suppressed anger (which probably was produced in you by your Muslim family) on people your religion rationalizes as deserving death for not being Muslim?

Another piece, under the headline 'The Pentagon breaks the Islam Taboo', states that 'a key Pentagon intelligence agency involved in homeland security is delving into Islam's holy texts to answer whether Islam is being radicalized by the terrorists or is already radical.'

Freedom of speech is a principle that cannot be compromised or given up. Yet writers and publications who correctly support Ayaan Hersi Ali's defence of this principle seem unable or unwilling to distinguish between defending the principle of free speech and acting as the handmaidens of hate and the dehumanization of a community. And when Muslims are offended by remarks made by people such as Ayaan Hersi Ali, when they are offended by being referred to as 'goat fuckers' or when they are offended by cartoons of the Prophet wearing a turban in the shape of a bomb, they are condemned, their protests defined as 'anti free speech'. But if people in prominent positions set out to provoke and offend, why are they so surprised when people feel provoked and offended?

The promotion of the views of Ayaan Hersi Ali stands in terrible contrast to the abandonment of the faceless and nameless victims of the violence and hate directed at Muslims. When Nick Griffin, the leader of the British National Party, urges people to decide whether Britain 'should become an Islamic Republic or a democracy' is he so very different from Ayaan Hersi Ali? Yet we condemn one as a fascist and we promote the other as a pioneer of free speech and a representative of the Muslim community in the West.

The fates of Yassin Hassan Omar and Ayaan Hersi Ali could not be more different, in the decisions they have made and the actions they have taken. However, in many ways their similarities outweigh their differences. They both came from a country destroyed by civil war, their families escaped to the West in the hope of starting a new life, yet both found themselves suddenly disconnected from their family and their past. Their experiences produced two starkly different, yet equally zealous responses, which in their own ways present the greatest threats to the hope that a place like Edgware Road symbolizes for the overwhelming majority of Muslims. Each of them embodies an absolute vision that comes directly from their individual experiences: in the case of Yassin Hassan Omar and his fellow suicide bombers it is an absolute rejection of the West; in Ayaan Hersi Ali's case it is an utter rejection of Islam. In both cases it is a rejection of the place where I spent nineteen years of my life, a place where Islam and the West co-exist. With equal ardour they both reject the only thing there is: hope.

2. Coming Home

I t was 1991 and the first Gulf War had just ended. At the same time, but with little of the same attention, the civil war and the famine that was its consequence were beginning in Somalia while the military dictatorship in neighbouring Ethiopia was on the brink of collapse following decades of civil war. I had not returned to Somalia for many years. While I was a teenager I had been far more interested in hanging around with my British friends, going to parties and generally doing what most teenagers do, than going back on long family visits to Somalia. Few Somalis were immigrating to Britain during the early 1980s which meant my family had only a small circle of Somali relatives and friends with whom to connect us to our old home. I was pretty much an English teenager and Islam and Africa seemed distant and part of an unfamiliar past. Most of my friends were not Somalis and not Muslims, and I had the same aspirations as them.

But as the war in the north of Somalia worsened through the 1980s, many more Somalis began to flee. Many of them were relatives and friends of my family. During those years our home was never quiet, our spare room never empty. Newly arrived old friends and relations would stay with us while we helped them fill out forms and register with the local authorities. There was a constant stream of visitors seeking company and reassurance. Until then, the war had been an abstract event made real only through small articles buried in the corner of the foreign news pages in newspapers and by occasional radio reports. Suddenly the war reconnected me with a part of myself. Close friends and family had lost everything, and hearing their stories made them and the war a part of my life for the first time.

In 1992 a university friend and I had planned a long trip to Asia, imagining ourselves as foreign correspondents, hoping to find a job on the way as stringers for an international news agency. We planned to fly to Hong Kong and write freelance articles as we travelled through South-east Asia, heading towards South and Central Asia. We bought our tickets and Edward went on ahead of me; I was to join him a month later. However, just after he left in May, the military dictatorship of Colonel Mengistu Haile Mariam in Ethiopia fell when a rebel coalition captured the capital Addis Ababa. The war in Somalia had been going on for four years and the collapse of the Ethiopian dictatorship made the Somali refugee camps in eastern Ethiopia more accessible. I knew I had to go. Over the past few years my interest in the war and my concern for what was happening had intensified dramatically. I was no longer a teenager and I felt strongly that I had to see for myself what had happened in Somalia. I had to see the camps where friends and relatives had been living before they arrived on our doorstep.

I returned to the travel agency near Victoria station, which catered for students looking for the cheapest flights around the world, with my ticket to Hong Kong in my hand. I wanted to fly to Addis Ababa instead. The same agent who had sold us the tickets a month earlier beckoned me over. When I told him what I wanted, he looked surprised. 'What about your friend,' he asked. 'Isn't he already out there expecting you?' I tried to brush him off with some excuse and reluctantly he changed my ticket, occasionally glancing up at me with a disapproving frown. He was right to look at me like that, I had let my friend down. When I phoned Edward to tell him I wasn't coming, his generous response made me feel worse. He said it was the best thing I could do. That new ticket changed my life.

In 1992 I was still a citizen of Somalia. Inside my green Somali passport was a black stamp declaring that the Home Office had given me permission to stay in the United Kingdom for an indefinite period. But the nation-state to which I really belonged existed only in name, and within a year it would disappear altogether. Mine was an odd existence. During my university years and my early twenties it was almost impossible for me to get a visa to travel outside Britain. About seven months earlier some friends and I decided at short notice to make a trip to France. I immediately went to the French embassy to apply for my visa. There I was asked what my nationality was. When I told them, they said it would take three weeks and I would need: a letter from my university to prove I had attended it; proof that I had the funds to support myself during my trip to France (I intended to stay only for a long weekend); a letter from someone stating they would vouch for me financially if I couldn't support myself during the trip; proof that I had a return ticket back to the

UK and a detailed list of where I was going to stay in France. The rules would have been the same for any European country I had wanted to visit. As long as Somalia was in a state of crisis we were all potential refugees, whoever we were and whatever our backgrounds.

Getting into Ethiopia would prove to be even trickier as thousands of destitute Somalis were arriving each week from across the vast and unpatrolled border along the Ogaden desert. Poor countries have to deal with the overwhelming majority of the world's refugees and asylum seekers. The numbers of refugees that African, Asian and Middle Eastern countries have had to cope with dwarfs the numbers faced by European countries. Iran has sheltered more Afghan refugees from the Taliban than all European countries combined. It has also taken in thousands of Iraqis who fled Saddam Hussein's dictatorship. It took me a month to get through the bureaucracy and suspicion before my request to extend my Ethiopian visa was granted.

The questions of the Ethiopian administration differed little from those of the French embassy in London. However, there was one key difference in the application process. In order to get to the refugee camps and then on to Somalia itself I needed the help of Western aid agencies and the principal United

Nations agency, the High Commission for Refugees (UNHCR). It was a sobering experience. I made the mistake of presuming that my very British accent, my education and my affluent appearance would be enough to protect me from the suspicion and humiliation that almost everyone else who carried the same passport as me faced. But this is not how things work if you come from a failed state, and I should have known better. The Ethiopian authorities and some of the aid agencies doubted the authenticity of my documents. As increasing numbers of Somalis sought exile in the West, ever more documents had to be produced to verify the authenticity of the documents I already had. I had to prove again that I was a freelance journalist. I was told that I should register at the UNHCR offices on arrival in Dire Dawa, the border town between Ethiopia and Somalia. Although I had grown up in Britain and believed myself as western as any young American or British graduate, my upbringing counted for nothing. The fact that I was carrying a Somali passport 'lowered' my status in their eyes. I felt stupid and arrogant for believing that I would be treated differently because of the privileges I had grown to take for granted in Britain.

I was reminded of the story of Gandhi's experience on a train in Natal, South Africa shortly after his arrival in the country from Britain where he had qualified as a barrister at the Inns of Court in London. He climbs into the compartment of a first-class carriage, unaware that the racial segregation laws of South Africa mean that he is supposed to travel in the compartments set aside for non-whites. He is told by an inspector to get out of the first-class carriage. He starts to explain that there has been a misunderstanding, that he is a lawyer in London and he really does have a first-class ticket, but before he has time to reach into his pocket for it, he is thrown off the train along with his luggage.

It took me about another week to get permission from the UNHCR and the Save the Children Fund to visit the refugee camps in the east, and to stay with them during my visit. As well as my Ethiopian visa extension papers, I was required to provide a letter from the BBC stating that I was researching a radio report for the Africa Service of the World Service.

Dire Dawa is the last main city in eastern Ethiopia before the empty, flat wilderness of the Ogaden desert. It feels like a frontier town, as you leave behind the gentle farming highlands of Christian Ethiopia and enter the flat, dry, hot plains of Ethiopia's Somali Muslim region and then Somalia itself. Dire Dawa is a gateway into Ethiopia for

Somali nomads and their produce, as well as a place where Western or locally manufactured consumer goods are sold to the rural and nomadic populations in the hinterland of the Ogaden and the open interior of Somalia. Even now nomads can be seen driving their herds of camels through the streets of the low-built town.

The station lies at the centre of the town on the southern edge of the main roundabout. The French built the railway at the end of the nineteenth century to provide access to the Ethiopian and Somali interior for the port of Djibouti, which was then a French colonial possession. The railway had been the lifeblood of the city, bringing goods and people from the principal towns of the region to the border to trade. The city is now served by a modest airport. However, there is one reason why Dire Dawa is not the unremarkable, dust-blown frontier town it might have been: along the walls of its ordered streets or like canopies over the sun-bleached houses hang great fountains of wild bougainvillea. The town is covered with it. It grows in public squares, in the courtyards of the many small, cheap guesthouses and along the roadsides. The blue, red, violet, orange, lilac and creamy white of the flowers contrast sharply with the dry plains that surround the city.

The droughts, wars and processions of displaced

people which have become the tragic story of the Horn of Africa over the past three decades have meant that an army of relief workers and consultants have been a permanent fixture in Dire Dawa for nearly thirty years. Their huge four-wheel-drive vehicles are now as natural a feature in eastern Ethiopia as camels. And just as camels crowd together near Dire Dawa's central market, Mitsubishis and Toyotas bristling with radio antennae are crammed together in the car parks of the best hotels and compounds. And now, among the nomads and their herds who have been passing through Dire Dawa for a century and the white Jeeps speeding past, there is a new gang in town. The American army has arrived. At first glance they are indistinguishable from the aid workers or missionaries in the uniform of the Westerner in Africa: rugged designer boots and ersatz khaki combat trousers with lots of pockets. But their haircuts give them away: the shaved back and sides and the short, neat, flat top of the head establishes them as members of the American armed forces. Small groups of US military personnel have been quietly posted to eastern Ethiopia in the years since September 11.

The Ogaden, the empty and largely uncharted territory between Ethiopia and Somalia, is one of the least visible and least reported frontlines in the so-called 'War on Terror'. For centuries it has been a region where the Muslim lowlands of eastern Ethiopia and Somalia and the Christian highlands of Ethiopia have rubbed up against each other. Somali oral tradition recounts that as far back as the beginning of the fourteenth century, the Sultan of a Muslim kingdom in what is now the Ogaden began a war against neighbouring Christian kingdoms in the highlands of what is now Ethiopia. But the tide turned, and the Abyssinian king, Yeshaq, routed Muslim forces and crushed all resistance as far as the Indian ocean port of Zeila, in present-day Somaliland. The historian I. M. Lewis claims in his book *A Modern History of the Somali Nation and State in the Horn of Africa* that it is in the songs celebrating Yeshaq's victories from this period that the word 'Somali' is recorded for the first time.

The sectarian wars between the Christian and Muslim communities of the region continued sporadically for centuries and were always a source of tension, exacerbated by economic competition for trade and livestock in land with scarce resources and little water. This political, cultural and religious mix provided the perfect conditions for charismatic clerics and tribal leaders to inspire and lead uprisings against colonial forces and influences from the late nineteenth century when Britain, France and Italy

partitioned Somalia and created their own protector-
ates. The most famous of these leaders was Sayyid
Mohammed Abdille Hassan. Even back then nick-
names for Muslim clerics were common and he was
no exception, known as he was by the colonial forces
as 'The Mad Mullah'. Some things never change.
Sayyid Mohammed's homeland was what is now the
self-declared Republic of Somaliland in the north.

Mohammed was born in the 1860s and, like every
other young Somali boy, began to learn the Quran
from an early age. He later travelled to the ancient
walled city of Harar, the home town of Yassin Omar,
the failed suicide bomber, in present-day eastern
Ethiopia, which is about fifty miles south of Dire
Dawa. Harar was part of an Islamic sultanate for
centuries and also a significant mercantile centre,
attracting Arab traders who had settled on the Indian
Ocean coast from the seventh century onwards.
Trade and contact with Arab settlers inevitably
brought not just conversion to Islam but also Islamic
learning, and so Harar became a significant seat
of Quranic study. Ever since that period Islamist
preachers, movements and political organizations
have had a presence in this region of eastern
Ethiopia. Some of the political groups in Harar have
used violence to promote their main political aim
of remaining as free as possible from political or

economic control by any authority in the area. The emptiness and remoteness of the vast region has allowed them to do this. It is also the reason why the US government has been monitoring the area. There are few places in the region where it is easier to evade detection and capture.

The road from Dire Dawa to Harar descends gradually from the last vestiges of the Ethiopian highlands to the plains of the Ogaden, yet in no more than an hour's drive, the changes are stark. It's not just that the mountains and escarpments give way to flat plains, or that the lush green fields and tall trees disappear or that the freshness of the mountain breeze gives way to a hot, dry wind. The change is also apparent in the faces of the people. Many Ethiopian men and women, especially in the east of the country, have the sign of the cross cut into their foreheads – just two small nicks with a razor blade. By the time you reach Harar very few faces are marked. Women wear long, brightly coloured robes and patterned shawls to cover their heads, and the men, instead of trousers, wear a *ma'awis*, a piece of cloth tied like a sarong around the waist, and their heads are almost completely covered by large skull-caps.

As you descend a little further beyond Harar, you reach a small town called Jigjiga. Although it lies within Ethiopia, it is close to the border with Somalia, which runs for hundreds of miles across empty and wild terrain, and is completely unguarded. Nomads come and go across this border. As a result it has the feel of an unregulated frontier town. And because it is in the lowland, largely Muslim part of Ethiopia, there is a greater Somali influence. In the last two decades Jigjiga has made its living off the border crossings – from nomads and traders bringing in livestock, gum and frankincense from Somalia and Ethiopians bringing consumer goods to transport into Somalia. It is a way station for truck drivers and traders to rest and refuel.

I arrived in Jigjiga on one of the communal minibuses which plies the route from Dire Dawa and is mainly used by Somalis. When I got off and asked for directions to the offices of a British aid agency, four people eagerly stepped forward to explain the route and tell me how long it would take to get there. So many of the town's inhabitants had tried to find work with the international aid agencies that everyone knew exactly where each one was based. The town of Jigjiga is an example of the enormous economic power humanitarian agencies wield in the regions where they operate and the distorting effect they can have on local economies: local doctors were often paid better to work as advisers and assistants to young Western medics than as doctors in local state clinics. A local merchant was better off hiring his equipment, generators or lorries to the aid agencies than to other businesses in the area who rely on them to survive.

There were four young British aid workers in the compound, served by nine or ten local staff: drivers, guards and assistants. There were many more at the main administrative office and warehouse in town and I wasn't about to count the cleaners and cooks who also served them. They led an incestuous life: gossiping about their colleagues in other agencies and whose turn it was to invite the others for a drink, which of the bars and hotels in town were the best places to hang out nowadays, and of course the most critical point of all, which of the agencies and their staff had been written about or interviewed by international journalists most recently. Publicity is the lifeblood of aid agencies. It's what guarantees their survival. They let me stay with them for the night and offered me a lift to the refugee camp the next morning, but I sensed that they realized I didn't represent much power in the international media despite my well-thumbed and creased letter of introduction from the BBC Africa Service.

Hartishek refugee camp is about thirty miles from Jigjiga. It is a place of huge significance for any

Somali from the north of the country, representing, as it does, the experience of war and exile for an entire nation. Few Somali families would not know someone who has passed through the camp. It did not just represent the loss and suffering which all wars bring, but was also the starting point from which our new lives in exile in the West can be traced. It was the place where people's sense of home ended and where a new Somali journey and story began – a journey of mass migration and a story which will take two generations to complete. Where ships and ports were the abiding images for British and Irish migrants 200 years ago, so refugee camps are the modern-day equivalent markers for large numbers of migrants to the West. In our age of mass migrations within Africa itself and from Africa, Asia and parts of the Middle East to the West, it is in the refugee camps scattered across these lands that the stories of these modern-day migrants begin.

Hartishek was built on the flat arid savannah plains of the border region between Ethiopia and northern Somalia. Somalis from Hargeisa and the refugees themselves know it by a different name, Dul'ad, which can mean 'white land' but literally translates as 'barren surface'. It is a reference to the fine dust that covers the land for miles. It is suffocating and gets everywhere. The slightest breeze, however welcome because of the heat, throws dust over everything. It filled my nose and throat and made me gag; it coated my eyebrows and eyelashes, the hair on my arms and on my head. Everyone in Dul'ad looks prematurely aged, their heads grey with dust. This harsh, empty land was home to over 300,000 refugees. There was no source of water nearby so water had to be trucked in by the aid genies from Jigjiga; no natural barriers to give shelter from the elements; no rocks or escarpments to provide shade from the heat of the day and offer protection from the near freezing temperatures at night; and there were no other permanent settlements near the camps. There was nothing to draw anyone here.

We came off the main road from Jigjiga and drove down a straight dusty lane which headed directly towards Hartishek. Empty lorries which had carried food supplies to the camps passed us, churning up clouds of dust which billowed into our vehicle. My eyes were glued to the road ahead. Over the last few years, during mealtimes at home, or when friends visited or newly arrived refugees came to stay, conversation would be filled with the stories from Hartishek. I was determined to remember for ever my first sight of the camp. We kept driving, but I saw nothing. Minutes passed without any sign of the camp where hundreds of thousands of men, women and children lived. Enormous warehouses where the food supplies were stored came into view, but where were the tents of the people? 'I don't understand, I can't see the camp,' I said to the aid worker driving the car. 'It's all around us,' he said. 'Look at the horizon.' He pointed his finger in a wide arc across the windscreen. I had expected the refugee camp to appear in front of me, huddled up along the side of the road. My vision changed and suddenly the landscape was transformed into a vast tented city, spreading and growing out of sight. Its scale was so vast, it was so fractured and scattered across the plain that I hadn't been able to see it at all.

I expected to see starving, helpless people rush up to our car or sit silently by the road waiting patiently for aid, dressed in filthy rags. However, when we got closer to some of the tents and I began to walk around between the makeshift homes I discovered shop owners and teachers, mechanics and builders, civil servants and nurses all trying to make for themselves a life that bore some resemblance to what they had left behind. Refugee camps are formed in response to a natural and unsurprising human instinct: to try to re-create the life and basic dignities you have suddenly and violently lost. In Hartishek men who had been tailors back in Somaliland had brought with them or bought pedal-driven sewing machines and had set up stalls under sheets of old cloth, supported by wooden poles. Barbers had bought a chair, a bucket and a pair of scissors with the small amounts of cash or jewellery that they had managed to carry with them when they fled their homes. It was a means of survival and a way of maintaining self-respect, to avoid having to wait meekly and helplessly for aid. People talk of refugees profiteering, or perhaps scenes like these make people think that such refugees are all right and don't need help. But hunger and disease lived here too.

I spent three nights at Hartishek, sharing the floor of one of the UNHCR's tarpaulin-covered warehouse with dozens of Ethiopian and Somali truck drivers and local camp officials. On the fourth day I got up at dawn to wait for one of the buses which took refugees across the border to Hargeisa. Refugees, too frightened to return home for good, often travelled back to see what they could recover from their homes, or to prevent squatters from moving into their damaged houses. There were others who, like me, had travelled from Britain and other European countries where there were growing Somali exile communities, to look up and help relatives, or just to find out what the war had done to their country.

The sun rose behind the growing crowd of people

waiting to set off for Hargeisa. The drivers would
not leave until they had a full load. Two young men
began to pile up the roof of the old bus with the
passengers' battered suitcases fastened together with
string and boxes filled with blankets, food, gas canisters. Then it was our turn to squeeze inside the bus.
I managed to find a seat on one of the hard wooden
benches and wondered how I was going to survive
the ten-hour journey across the savannah plains.
But as soon as the driver started up the engine the
excitement of the passengers took over. A middle-
aged man at the back of the bus shouted out: '*Bis-
millahi Rahmani Rahim*', 'In the Name of God,
the Compassionate, the Merciful', the prayer used
by Muslims at the beginning of a journey. The other
passengers joined in and the refrain echoed around
the vehicle as we pulled away from the central
market of the refugee camp.

There were no roads or markings or signs. There
were only the endless white plains with the occasional thorn bush or tree. The drivers of these buses,
themselves refugees, know the way from memory,
and also from shared experience. After each trip
drivers exchange information about dangers and
threats they have either encountered themselves or
have heard of from nomads they have met along the
way. Landmines left over from the war were the

biggest threat then, and flash floods could transform a dry river bed into an impassable quagmire. The drivers followed a map inside their heads, guided only by landmarks such as clusters of trees, low sandbanks, bends in dry river beds, the direction of distant hills.

From the beginning of the journey the bus was filled with chatter. Somali culture is very informal and it is quite usual for strangers to approach each other and talk as if they've been acquainted for years. Men of all ages greet each other with '*Waryaa*'. It's a command that can loosely be translated as 'Tell me!' Women say '*Nayaa!*', which means the same thing. Somalis ask personal questions of each other from the outset: who are your parents and where are they from? Which clan do you belong to? So many of us were travelling back to Somaliland harbouring the same feelings of hope and fear – it was as if we were all looking for reassurance from each other. We quickly forgot about our discomfort and the thought of the ten hours squashed up against our fellow passengers. 'Where are you from?' the man next to me asked. Then an older woman who was eavesdropping joined the conversation. 'Oh, I have a niece who went to Britain over a year ago. But she isn't living in London, she's in a town called Sheffield, where she says there is a large Somali population. She says that it is quite hard to get into college in Britain. Is that true? Is it difficult? Do you have to pay a lot of money for a college education?' She told us she was now living in Norway and that life for refugees was very good, apart from the cold. Suddenly a man sitting nearby pointed out of the window into the distance and shouted, 'Do you remember that place? That was the place the *faqash* [slang for General Siad Barre's military dictatorship] used helicopters to attack crowds of people who were fleeing their homes.' Several passengers murmured that they had heard the same story. 'We are rid of them now,' one woman said, 'may God curse them until eternity.'

By the late afternoon we were drawing close to the outskirts of Hargeisa, the capital of the self-declared Republic of Somaliland. The bus climbed steadily up the escarpment on which the city rests, nearly 4,000 feet above sea level. We were leaving the empty wilderness of the savannah and beginning to see the first signs of urban settlement; the water-pumping facilities and the electricity sub-stations about twenty miles from the city lay abandoned and in ruins. The walls and roofs seemed to have been blown apart. The excitement around me died away and the bus fell silent. Everybody stared out of the windows. The citrus farms on the edge of Hargeisa had been destroyed; only a few spindly trees were left standing. On the tarmac road into the city, our bus began to bump along the craters and cracks created by the tracks of tanks and destruction was evident wherever we looked. Perhaps I under-estimated the devastation because Hargeisa had been a small and relatively poor city to begin with. Had its houses and offices been built with cheap materi-als? Or was the destruction of the town so great because the civilian population and the rudiment-arily armed opposition group had been impotent against a military dictatorship whose MIG aircraft took off every day from the city's airport to bomb the city itself?

The main road into the city continues straight on, leading to the small market district. Bullet holes punctured every surface; even the street lamp posts were honeycombed with shrapnel holes. There was complete silence in the bus for what felt like an hour but, when I looked out of the window, I realized it could only have been a few minutes.

Before I had left London my parents and the rest of my family had given me detailed instructions about what I should do once I reached Hargeisa. My parents still held a map of their home town in their heads, more than twenty years after they had left. They told me I should head for the Geed Deeble

Motel, which was on the high street in Hargeisa. It was owned by my uncle Osman Samater and his wife, whose six children I had grown up with in Mogadishu, but whom I hadn't seen for ten years. Looking back now, I understand how brave it was of my parents to allow me to go back on my own to what was still a very dangerous place. They realized how much I needed to witness what had happened.

I got off the bus along with a few other passengers near one of the main squares. I asked if any of them knew where the Geed Deeble Motel was and one of them gave me directions. The motel was one of the few businesses still operating in its neighbourhood. Outside the entrance three young men sat behind a broken cabinet which was serving as a makeshift reception desk. '*Salaam Alaikum*, can we help you?' they asked. I said I was looking for Mohammed Osman Samater. The young man nearest to me eyed me curiously. 'Who can I say you are?' I was loath to give my full patrilineal name which would have immediately identified me, my family and the clan I belong to. 'My name is Rageh Abdullahi,' I said. 'Rageh Abdullahi who?' he replied. 'Well, I'm just a relative of his. He'll know who I am if you just tell him that.' He wouldn't let go. 'Just give me your full name,' he insisted. This game continued for a while before I broke in frustration.

'OK, my name is Rageh Abdullahi Omaar.' The young man smiled broadly. 'You don't recognize me, and I didn't think you'd be here for a few more days. It's me, Mohammed.' Osman's eldest son, my first cousin whom I'd played with as a child, was the first person I met in the wreckage of Hargeisa.

The following day Osman took me to my parents' house, which stands at one of the main junctions in the centre of town. My father built our house at the beginning of the 1960s. Across the street is what is still the city's only general hospital, where my oldest sister was born. Next door to the hospital, and on the street corner perpendicular to our house are the offices of the main radio station. Five minutes' walk away is the presidential compound. By the time I was born, my family had already moved from Hargeisa to Mogadishu, the capital of what was then the unified Republic of Somaliland, and so I had never seen the house and had no idea of what to expect. On our way there my uncle had mentioned vaguely that some families were temporarily living there, but that I was not to worry in the slightest. He tapped politely but authoritatively on the imposing wrought-iron door. A man opened it slightly and looked at us warily. '*Salaam Alaikum*, how are you?' my uncle said firmly. The two men had clearly met before. 'This is Rageh Abdullahi Omaar, whose father owns this property. The family may decide to return some time in the near future, and so he has come round to inspect the place.' The man peering from behind the large double metal door seemed reassured. He must have been worried that we were another family who wanted to move in as squatters. The fact that my family were the owners but only wanted to see what state the house was in at least meant that he and his family wouldn't have to sleep rough in the remains of one of Hargeisa's bombed-out houses. 'You're welcome,' he said meekly, 'please do come in.' He opened the gate to let us enter, then shut it quickly behind us.

I was seeing the house for the first time. I was amazed that it had not been hit by the artillery barrages and aerial bombing that the Siad Barre dictatorship had subjected Hargeisa to so indiscriminately. The solid outer walls of the low, wide villa were decorated with large, roughly cut pieces of brightly coloured local stone. Sitting in the middle of an acre of land the main house is surrounded by patches of lawn and clumps of apple trees that provide welcome shade. When we walked inside we discovered that it had been stripped of most of its contents. On the floor were three mattresses owned by the squatter, his wife and small children. At the back of the house the squatter's wife was washing pots and pans in a bucket. I tried my best to reassure the man that I had not come to drive him out. I thanked him awkwardly for looking after the house, and immediately felt self-conscious. The truth was that the arrangement served our respective families well, but at that moment the difference in our circumstances seemed unbearable. I walked around taking photographs to take back to my parents in London. It had been here, in this empty, dilapidated house that my father had begun his business which would eventually take us to the West. My father had married my mother here and started a family. My brother and sisters had all been born and brought up in this house, and now I was able to see it for myself.

My parents were eventually able to return to their house and they live there now. They can have their British grandchildren to stay in this house so full of memories because it was protected by a family who had themselves lost everything.

I drove through the unfamiliar streets of Hounslow on the western edge of London, following Ahmed's car. Ahmed's family have been lifelong friends of my family. He came to Britain from the place I had visited thirteen years earlier; through the Ogaden and through months of despair in Hartishek refugee camp. Today he works with local and national government

bodies and local Somali community groups on problems such as educational underachievement and
young offenders. We were on our way to visit family
friends. I followed Ahmed into a close of small
modern houses and tidy front gardens and parked.
As we got out of our cars an aeroplane roared overhead on its final approach to Heathrow airport, only
a mile or so away. It was so close I could see the tyres
and hydraulic pumps of the plane's undercarriage.

A young woman in her twenties opened the door
to us. She was dressed in a long Islamic gown, her
head covered in a shawl to hide her hair. We greeted
her in the traditional way by touching our chests
rather than reaching out to shake her hand, and she
showed us through the hall to the neat sitting room.
Islamic posters were hung on the walls. The largest
picture was a bird's eye view of the Grand Mosque
in Mecca at night, the magnificent pillars lit up by
hundreds of carefully directed lights. At the centre
of the image stood the large black building of the
ka'aba at the heart of the shrine. On the far wall
attached by thumbtacks were two black and white
scrolls inscribed with verses from the Quran, asking
God to bless the house and the family who lived in
it. A woman's voice called out to the girl who had led
us in. 'Have you offered them some tea?' she asked.

Samia Mohammed Aden walked in, smiling

broadly. Like her daughter she wore a full-length Islamic dress and a shawl covering her hair. She enquired after my family: my mother and, in particular, my father's health. She had heard that I had been to Hargeisa the previous summer with my wife and children and was curious to know how my children, then aged four and two and who had grown up in London, had adapted to life in Hargeisa where we had spent a month's holiday. Like all children at that age, all they noticed was the freedom they had to explore and run around, racing through orchards and watching goats graze along pavements in the middle of the city and nomads bringing camels to market – and being spoiled by dozens of adoring relatives. They did not notice the poverty or the fact that virtually everyone was black or that some buildings on the outskirts of town were riddled with bullet holes.

'That's wonderful,' Samia said, 'it's always wonderful to see Somali children who have grown up in Britain react in the same way when they return to visit relatives each year.' Then she told me that she had seen my older sister, Rakiya, in Hargeisa only two months earlier. I remarked on how small our world was. 'It's even smaller when you are Somali and Muslim living in Britain at the moment!' she joked.

Samia had heard that I wanted to write about our lives in Britain and she was pleased. But there was something about the way she spoke which suggested that she had seen too much and experienced too much to allow her to be too hopeful. We can hope, she seemed to be saying, but as Muslims it will take us generations to be accepted as British, no matter how hard we try.

We talked about Somalia and she began to describe her life before the war began in Hargeisa. 'My name is Samia Mohammed Aden,' she said. 'I would like to tell the story of Hargeisa, where I was born, where I went to school. I am one of those people who belonged to the land. I was married there and I had my children there. Hargeisa has all of my roots and I was forced to flee it. All of us in the city faced the same inescapable question,' she continued. '"How can we continue to live here?" We all wanted to. None of us wanted to leave. But we faced so many questions and difficulties.'

The dictator Siad Barre had faced growing opposition to his rule in northern Somalia and its main city, Hargeisa. Throughout the military dictatorship's existence and the transformation of Somalia into a one-party state, security organizations proliferated and gross human rights violations became common. Many methods were used to destroy any opposition to the regime; imprisonment and torture based on mere suspicion or the confessions of others who had been tortured, exile, confiscation of property and businesses, intimidation of relatives. Organizations sprang up around the country dedicated to the overthrow of the regime; the clans of those regions were systematically persecuted. There were mobile treason courts which dispensed summary justice against those who had been accused of not supporting the regime. In Hargeisa, the Isaak, the predominant clan, and the clan to which I and my family belong, were regarded by the regime as its most dangerous internal enemy after the formation of the Somali National Movement (SNM), a political and military organization aimed at overthrowing the regime.

By the mid-1980s, as the SNM guerrillas gained control of more and more of the interior, the regime's forces were left holding only the main cities. The war would eventually be fought in the cities, most ferociously in Hargeisa. 'There were so many things that we could and could not do according to the regime which was trying to intimidate everyone in Hargeisa because we were from a different clan from them,' Samia said. 'So many of the men had fled to join the rebels that many households were left only to the women. My husband was working in Abu Dhabi at the time, sending back money for me and the children. The electricity to our districts would often be cut and so we had only the gas canisters for lighting when the soldiers conducted their regular raids. They had no decency or civility. Quite the opposite. That's why it was so effective, because it was brutal. They would shout even louder when they saw children were there, to make everyone even more afraid. They would throw everything around, saying they were looking for weapons and guns.'

Samia's face changed, and she raised her eyebrows as she remembered an important point. 'But despite all this, we were the lucky ones because they never took much from us. But when the raids in the neighbourhood had finished we would sometimes hear screams and wailing from the houses of neighbours and we would all come running. You would ask, "What's happened?", and people would say, "They've taken my jewellery and our money."' This was not only about the anguish of being robbed of precious possessions. It was also about survival. Jewellery and money were the only things people knew they would be able to rely on when the moment to flee came. Their theft was not simply an act of petty and cruel self-enrichment by individual soldiers, it made escape almost impossible. 'To argue or complain meant you and your family risked being marked out,' Samia went on, 'no one could protect you from them, they had power over everything. They closed schools, they banned mosques and they curtailed prayers. Evening prayers, usually at five or six o'clock, were banned because of the curfew. They even subjected God to curfew!'

They assaulted local culture too. In Somali culture weddings are huge affairs. Families hire ballrooms and halls for the celebrations, having saved up, often for years, in order to be able to entertain friends and family lavishly. Everyone dresses up in their finest, including the youngest children. Weddings were always held in the evenings to avoid the heat, but the ban on all evening activity and the curfew ended this. Weddings had to be held during the day. 'It may sound like a little thing, but it ruined people's big day, the chance for a bit of happiness. As you know, the brides are dressed and made up over hours. Their hands are painted with henna, a big fuss is made. And our country is very hot during the day, people stay in during the midday heat. With the weddings in the day the bride's make-up was ruined by the heat and sweat, the children found it unbearable. It was just miserable, and so humiliating.'

Samia said that everyone knew that the war was

imminent. The SNM fighters came ever closer to Hargeisa. 'None of us had ever witnessed war and because of that we were unaware of the reality, we spent our time welcoming it, thinking it would end the dictatorship and free us and we could be happy again. We believed there was no alternative to war and we welcomed it.' She smiled sadly. 'How naïve! But in truth, once it began, and we tasted what war was . . .' She didn't finish the sentence. 'No one who has truly seen war would wish it or welcome it. It's not an experience I can easily retell. Even now, in my life here in Britain, far away from the experience, with years having gone by, a certain noise, a certain smell or sound which I last experienced in my home in Africa makes me jump out of my skin.'

Like everyone else in the city, Samia had heard rumours that the SNM was going to enter Hargeisa at the end of May 1988. They had just attacked another major town, Burao, on 27 May, and it would not be long before the regional capital of Hargeisa was next. Families began frantically to stock up. It took Samia two days to buy as many items as she could that she thought would be useful in a time of siege. Men did not go out to search for provisions in Hargeisa's shops and markets. To do so would have been a sign to the security forces that people were preparing for the SNM attack and that would have meant certain arrest, and probably worse. 'Food, something light for the children to sleep on and which we could carry, charcoal, gas canisters. I bought them all. By the end my house looked like a small shop.' Then everyone was left to wait. The slow and seemingly endless wait for the war to start. Those last hours before a war breaks out remain with you for ever. They are the last hours that your home is as you have always known it, the last hours that your family lives in it, the last hours that your life is as it has always been.

'It began at two o'clock in the morning of 31 May. Boom, boom, boom,' Samia held her hands up and began to shake them furiously as she imitated the sound of the explosions. 'It was so loud.' Then, curiously, she smiles. 'But at that moment I and almost everyone else I knew, felt such joy. Of course we had no idea what lay ahead, but at that moment it just seemed that this hated and terrible regime was going to be ended and the suffering we had known would soon be over. I started saying prayers for the people of the city and for the rebels who had come to free us. But this is not how it happened.'

Samia and her three children – Mohammed, who was seven, and the two girls, Fathumo, who was six, and Asha, who was five months old – stayed in their house during the siege. A day after it began, as explosions from the bombardment could be heard across the city, there was a terrible sound of screaming. 'Some of our windows had been blown out, but I could not tell that it was due to an explosion very near us. The screams came from the house opposite ours – four or five adults screaming and wailing hysterically. Everyone in the neighbourhood, who until that moment had stayed inside, came running out. What had happened? A bomb or mortar had hit the house of the family opposite and one of the elderly men of the family had lost a leg. That was when all my illusions were destroyed. I knew then, at that very moment, that this war was not going to happen in the way we had all fooled ourselves that it would.'

She paused for a moment, and looked at me intensely. 'Whenever I now hear politicians and people who have never experienced war promise and proclaim that a particular conflict will deliver peace, that it will bring a terrible regime to an end and that it will all happen quickly and it will all be for the best, especially for ordinary people, I realize that for such people, there is a part of their sensitivity and imagination which is dead. They are incapable of imagining themselves as other people.' The ironic thing, Samia said, is that having stored so much food and provisions, none of them could eat. One reason was fear. 'That kind of fear kills your ability to think about other things: am I hungry? Am I thirsty? You forget you have such needs and feelings.' The other reason, she said, was hygiene. 'We lived in just one room of the house, and so our waste as well, urine and faeces, piled up in the next-door room. We tried to keep the smell out, but there was only so much we could do. We tried to avoid going outside with all the stray bullets everywhere, anything could have happened. The few times we had to venture to neighbours' houses, we saw corpses on some of the streets.'

Samia said she noticed a sudden change in the people around her in those first days of the war. 'People realized that this was going to be a long and horrifying experience. All the rejoicing and welcoming of the war was now a distant memory. We all had to confront something we had never prepared for. Many people started to pray and would read the Quran the whole time; the young and old, those who hadn't prayed in years as well as those of us who did. We started to pray.' I asked her what people prayed for. 'Many things, some people prayed because they had lost all other hope. They would say things like: "God, if I am to die, please let it be without suffering and pain, and spare my family";

others used it as a source of courage and strength for their families, to be able to bear the hardships. For them they were asking God for strength in this battle against an apostate government which was killing innocent Muslims. It varied, but our religion is there for us whatever we are feeling, and people reached for it in many different ways.'

Samia lived in the district called Goljano, which is near to my parents' house. By the eighth day, the SNM forces had effectively taken the area and government forces had retreated. On the ninth day Samia decided they had to leave. 'I packed only the barest essentials that I and the children could carry. I carried Asha on my back with a sheet strapping her tightly to me. I tied sheets and small blankets on to Mohammed and Fathumo's backs and they carried water.' Just before they left, Samia said to Mohammed and Fathumo, 'Listen to me very carefully. We are going to leave as quickly as possible and we will probably find many other families doing the same thing on the roads out of the city. But the journey to the outskirts of the town will be very, very dangerous. I want you to hear me when I say this: whatever God wills will happen. If anyone of us or any other person is hit you *must* keep running with whoever is left or with the other families. Those who die, will die, those that live must stay alive.' At the age of seven and five Mohammed and Fathumo had already seen corpses in the streets of their neighbourhood.

Samia and her children stayed behind the rebel lines and away from government forces who were bombing the city. They met hundreds of others on the road, like them carrying all their worldly possessions on their backs, on their heads and in their hands. 'As we moved through ravaged neighbourhoods, constantly listening out for any bombardment, the streets of central Hargeisa looked like a ghost town. But as we made our way through the different districts, occasionally the doors to houses which we thought were long abandoned began to creak open. From behind them, the faces of families who had been hiding and were too scared to go outside, in the same way that I had been only a few days earlier, began to appear. Seeing others on the move and fleeing gave them courage and these families asked if we could wait for them so they could join us on the march out of the city.'

By that evening, Samia and her children had left the outskirts of town and reached a water-pumping facility built by the Chinese in the 1970s. It marked the point where the urban areas around Hargeisa ended and the emptiness of the hinterland towards the Ethiopian border began. But reaching the safety of the empty plains of the Ogaden presented new problems because, like so many other middle-class refugees around the world, Samia and her children were completely unprepared for survival in the bleak wilderness of no man's land. 'When we arrived at the water-pumping station, it began to rain,' Samia recalled. 'Of course there was nowhere to escape from the rain, none of the buildings and shops and shelters which one finds in cities and towns. As a result we got wet.' She chuckled as she remembered what happened next. 'Then, my two eldest children turned to me and said, "Mummy can we have a change of clothes, we're wet," and I thought to myself, What change of clothes? We haven't got any clothes except for what we're all wearing!' She began to laugh heartily. 'At that moment, it suddenly seemed so funny.'

They had escaped the war in Hargeisa, but now had to do battle with the elements. The privilege, knowledge and sophistication of their urban life as the educated middle classes counted for nothing in the wilderness. They were still in their own country but felt as though they had stepped into an alien land. 'But, of course, you must remember,' Samia said, 'we still believed that the war would be over soon and we would be returning back to Hargeisa. Even though I had accepted the need to flee my home, for me it still didn't follow that I would leave for a new life in a new land, in a new culture.' Samia held on to this hope for two months. She and her children walked further into the bush and lived in the wilderness, making do with the meagre provisions they had brought with them, clubbing together with other families who had travelled with them from the city. They all believed they would be returning to Hargeisa soon and therefore there was no point in moving too far away, certainly not as far away as across the border into Ethiopia. But as the sick, elderly and very young got weaker and the risk of disease grew stronger people realized that they had no other choice but to try to reach a main town where they could receive sanctuary and relief, and that meant only one thing: escape into Ethiopia. Crossing an internationally recognized border formally made them refugees in the eyes of international humanitarian law, as opposed to simply being classified as 'internally displaced people' within their own countries. That was the route to Hartishek.

Samia's good fortune was that she had extended family in Dire Dawa and also in Britain. She spent the last remnants of the cash she had managed to save on a taxi to take her and her children to the outskirts of Dire Dawa where a distant cousin lived.

Arrival in Dire Dawa was the point at which she finally broke down and wept after the months of struggling to survive from minute to minute and to cope with the responsibility of ensuring that her children survived as well.

'We were covered in the fine dust of the Ogaden plains, and we were infested with lice after so long in the bush. After everything we had been through we had forgotten how we must have looked to people in a big town. We just presumed we were the same middle-class people who had fled Hargeisa but who had just been through a lot of hardship. We knocked on the metal gate of my relative's house. The watchman came to the door. Before I could say anything, he addressed me curtly, "Sorry we have no money today," and then closed the door. I banged on the gate again,' Samia continued, 'but he didn't bother to return to open it. "I've told you, we don't have anything, stop behaving like this and harassing people in their own homes." That hit me very hard. My children looked at me and asked why the man was saying those things, and I just began to weep. All I could think of,' she said, 'was that people were seeing us as vagrants and beggars; they could not recognize us any more as the ordinary family that we had been just a few weeks ago.'

It would take Samia's relatives in Britain a further five months to complete the paperwork so she was able to join them as a refugee. She and the children arrived in Britain on 14 January 1989, at Heathrow airport, which now, after all these years, is only a twenty-minute drive away. 'That day, a cold, cold, cold day, was the first time I had ever seen Britain.' Samia's children were full of questions. 'My daughter Fathumo wanted to know where we were going. "Mother, do we own a house in Britain?" "No," I replied. "Do you know where we are going to be staying?" "No, I don't, but God will provide us with something." My daughter thought about this and then she said, "If we don't own a house here and we don't know where we are staying, does that mean that we will be sleeping in the bush again?" A short while later, my son Mohammed turned to me and asked, "Is there fighting in Britain?" I took him by the shoulder and said, "No, there is no fighting here."'

Having been granted asylum, Samia and the children were sent by social services to a bed-and-breakfast in Earl's Court until accommodation was found for them. For the first time they felt at ease and finally safe. One of Samia's clearest memories from those days is of a meeting she had with a social worker who had become quite a friend in a short space of time. 'She asked me when I thought I would be returning home to Hargeisa and Somalia,' Samia said, 'and I wanted to give the most pessimistic prediction so I told the lady that I thought I would be able to return in two years' time.' Samia, Ahmed and I all burst out laughing.

Samia's children have been educated in this country, they are British citizens and will soon all be graduates of British colleges. From the horror and tragedy of their experience has emerged a family who are just as British as anyone else. And just as they feel proud and blessed to have achieved so much, proud of their new life and blessed that they are safe, it feels right that Britain should feel proud too to have such courageous, tough and dignified people. How lucky to have so many of the poor world's best and brightest, to have inherited those who should have been the teachers, doctors, lawyers and businessmen of countries such as Somalia, Afghanistan and Sierra Leone. Wars force people from their homes, and make them go in search of where home is or, at least, what home means. If we understand home as being a place which holds our memories and ties us to those we love, then home is a constantly changing place; always shifting with the circumstances and the stages in our lives. And just as we must change to fit our new homes and our new worlds, those worlds cannot but change too. My parents may be in Hargeisa now and Samia and her children may be in Hounslow, but both Britain and Somalia have shaped them, both places have given them – and me – a home.

3. Pilgrimages and Journeys

In 1972 my parents moved from Somalia to settle in Britain. My older brother and three sisters had already begun their studies there. It was to have been a temporary arrangement. My parents' first idea was to leave my older siblings in the UK during the school term, looked after by a guardian, and have them return to Somalia in the school holidays. In the meantime my father would visit them during his regular business trips to Europe. But then they decided that I too should be educated in Britain and the plans changed completely. My parents were not going to stay in Somalia while all their children grew up in a foreign land miles away. They did not want a life of emotional and physical commuting between continents and so they chose to move the whole family to Britain until we were all ready to return to Somalia. It was this journey out of Somalia that would come to define my parents so clearly in my mind and, even more so, it was their first journey out of Britain, on a pilgrimage to Mecca, that lives with me still and has such a bearing on how we as a family were brought up and how we see ourselves to this day.

The journey to join my older siblings in London would be my first trip outside the country of my birth. Until then, my upbringing revolved around our large, comfortable and crowded house in the capital, Mogadishu. Neighbours and relatives would drop by unannounced; the idea of arranging meetings in advance or booking appointments was unheard of in Somalia then and pretty much still is today, even among second-generation Somalis living in Britain. My mother is the oldest of seven sisters and the first of them to start a family. She was able to turn to her sisters for help in bringing up her children, just as millions of other young mothers do every day in Africa and the rest of the developing world. As most of my brothers and sisters were well past infancy by the time I was born I often had the undivided attention of my many aunts. However, even if our house by the sea was always crowded, I do also remember feeling the absence of my older brother and two eldest sisters who were approaching secondary-school age when I was a small toddler. I was delighted to discover, at the age of five, that I would be joining them.

Emigrating and settling in a new country is not something that happens quickly or easily. When we think of third-world immigrants travelling to the West we picture young, mostly male Africans crammed on to barely sailable boats, spending their days in dirt and squalor until they pitch up off the coasts of Italy or Greece. They could be a twenty-first-century version of the slave boats that took many of these young men's forefathers to America. Then there are the images of asylum seekers, of people being dragged out from their hiding places in the backs of lorries that have just emerged from the Channel tunnel from France to Britain. This is the reality for many people. However, immigration, whether legal or illegal, is not just about the desperate weeks on board a crowded boat or the stowing away in a container, or, if you're a middle-class immigrant, the overcrowded flight from Africa or Asia.

What these snapshots fail to capture are the long waits, the agonizing and often impenetrable bureaucracy, the uncertainty that immigration from one world to another always involves. They do not show the months of planning that are essential if you are bringing your family with you or, indeed, leaving many of them behind. They give no measure of the time it takes to raise the money for the trip, and how much money is required. The risks taken to raise funds are worse for those who have to borrow from gangs and pay people-smugglers, but middle-class families from a trading or professional background also face a long-drawn-out process to make sure that the relative who is seeking to go to the West has enough money not only to get there, but to ensure survival in the first months of their new life, with a place to live and food to eat until they find their feet or the help of other distant relatives already settled in the new country. And what do you do about those you leave behind?

The vast majority of people who travel to the West are those still young enough to hope that they can start a new life. They are usually men and women between the ages of twenty and forty, the most economically productive generation in any society. They leave behind parents, grandparents, uncles and aunts and sometimes their own young children who will be cared for by older relatives. Before they leave, those who have decided to emigrate have to satisfy themselves that their elderly relatives and dependants have some means of support. Which family member will keep an eye on things, who will take over responsibility for the family shop, or the plot of land? Who will guarantee that the children continue their schooling? The act of leaving affects dozens of people and these questions have to be answered before the immigrant even thinks of boarding a boat or stepping on to an aeroplane.

For most travellers from countries in Africa in the decade after independence, flying anywhere meant first stopping off in the capital of the country's former colonial ruler. Even today, more than forty years after the end of colonialism in most of Africa, it is often easier or cheaper to fly from West Africa to South Africa via Paris or Brussels than it is to fly direct. In 1972 travelling from Mogadishu to Britain meant flying first to Italy. Rome was my first experience of Europe. On our first night in the city I came down with a heavy cold and chesty cough, an ailment that was rare in the tropical balm of the Indian Ocean coast and probably a result of my first long-haul flight. It was late at night and the pharmacy near the hotel was closed. I could hear my mother and father running up and down the stairs to the receptionist who was trying to find a chemist willing to open up. I remember how strange it felt to be left entirely on my own, in our hotel bedroom. In Somalia it would be very unusual for a sick child not to be surrounded and fussed over by many people, family and friends; in my case, by a multitude of aunts.

Another surprise was in store for me when I finally recovered. We set off for a walk around the city and as we turned the corner of the street beside our hotel I stopped in my tracks. There, in front of me, standing in the centre of the cobbled square, was the strangest thing I had ever seen. Towering above us was an enormous fountain. Water poured from the mouths of its huge, naked stone figures. I cannot remember whether I was more amazed by the nakedness of the statues or by the waste of so much water.

A few days later we arrived in Heathrow to a new life. My parents had always believed that our stay in Britain would be long; perhaps ten or more years, but they never thought it was going to be for ever. Yet I think somewhere deep within themselves they did occasionally imagine a permanent life in Britain. I've always felt that even if my parents could not visualize or put their feelings into words they did realize that they had made a hugely important decision. I believe this because of what they did next.

A few months after we arrived in Britain my parents had to return to Somalia, to oversee the long process of settling all their affairs before we put down roots properly. Even though my family was emigrating from a privileged and comfortable position there were still things to be organized back home. But we did not return to Somalia via Italy. Instead my parents took me home via Saudi Arabia in order that they could perform the pilgrimage to Mecca. Why did they do that? Why did they choose that moment to go to Mecca, that moment to re-affirm their commitment to Islam? My parents' decision to perform the Hajj pilgrimage to Mecca at that time was inextricably linked with their decision to move their lives and children to a foreign country. Whether the two decisions were taken separately or not, they are tied together in the identity of my parents. They would have been concerned that leaving Somalia would take them away from the roots of their faith and culture. Could they be Western and Muslim? What would happen to their children growing up in a foreign country? I believe that somewhere deep within them my parents were beginning to wrestle with those questions. And now, nearly thirty years later, the same questions are haunting millions of other Muslims across Europe.

★

The meaning and symbolism of the pilgrimage to Mecca is central to the religion of Islam and lies at the heart of its practice. Many of the world's estimated 2 billion Muslims turn towards the direction of Mecca to perform their five daily prayers. One of the Five Pillars of Islam states that it is incumbent on all Muslims who are financially and physically able to make the pilgrimage to Mecca at least once in their lives. But the importance of the Hajj goes far beyond its role in the symbolism and tenets of Islam. The Hajj is the living example of what Muslims describe as the '*Ummah*' or the 'nation of believers'. It refers to a belief in a global and unified community of Muslims, who, whatever their language, skin colour, or tribal and national affiliations owe their first loyalty to their identity as Muslims. It is a concept that has held true among Muslims since the founding of the faith of the Prophet Mohammed. The pilgrimage to Mecca is the living embodiment of this idea. My parents' pilgrimage in 1972 was an attempt to reassure themselves that being part of the West would not mean they would lose a part of themselves, their heritage, their past, their tradition – that they or their children would not become less Muslim.

I remember the light at dusk. A sharp, pink glow in the sky dimming as it fell towards the earth, turning the plains golden brown as it sank beneath Mount Arafat. I remember the sea of pilgrims surging out of Mecca earlier in the day. I remember thousands of tents, the whites of their sheets dulled by the sand and dust from the desert around the Valley of Mina, the place where the Prophet Mohammed is said to have rested when he undertook the pilgrimage to Mecca. Today, this is the place where approximately 2 million Muslims from around the world spend the evening before the most important day of the Hajj. At dawn the following morning begins the biggest and most intense regular human migration on earth – on Thw Hajja, the last month of the Islamic lunar calendar. I remember the crowds walking out from the Valley of Mina. Some were crammed into buses and cars but most walked; hundreds of thousands of people following each other in lines across the desert towards Arafat, eight miles east of Mina. It was like a huge white tide spilling across the desert floor. The pilgrims, both men and women, were dressed in the *ihram*, a gown made of simple, pure white seamless cotton. Everyone wore sandals.

Arafat is where Muslims believe that the Prophet Adam and Hawa (Eve) were reunited and forgiven by God after a 200-year exile from Paradise. As the pilgrims make their way towards the small sacred

mountain, they chant aloud the prayer that is central
to the meaning and experience of the Hajj. The
'Talbiya' is a covenant, a declaration of purpose and
a commitment. It is also a prayer that strips to its
essence the word 'Islam', which means to submit to
God. The pilgrims chant out the words: 'Here I am
at your service O Lord. Here I am. Here I am at
your service and Thou hast no equals. All Praise and
All Bounty is Yours alone, and Yours alone is The
Sovereignty. Thou hast no equals.' I did not know
what the words meant or their significance when I
heard them. But I remember the loud shouts and
exultations ringing out as my parents and I joined
the procession. I remember feeling worried when I
saw the adults around me begin to cry. I remember
my mother holding me against the rough white cloth
of her *ihram*.

Once the pilgrims enter the boundary of Arafat
they begin what is one of the most moving, important but also tumultuous episodes of the Hajj.
Hundreds of thousands of pilgrims try to find a spot
of craggy desert ground on which to sit and briefly
rest. Even today, when the amenities provided for
the pilgrims have been renovated to a degree unimaginable at the time when my parents took me as
a child, people become separated and lost in the
crowds, and old people can die in the exhaustion

and crush. And yet, amid all this, many hundreds of thousands are undergoing an intense spiritual experience.

The experience at Arafat is viewed by Muslims as a preparation for Judgement Day. It is seen as a glimpse of what the Quran calls 'Yaum Al Qiyamah' which literally means 'The Day of Resurrection' but is also known as 'The Day of the Reckoning' when all mankind will be gathered on an unending white, featureless ground, with the blazing sun hovering overhead and where they will be called to account before Allah for their lives. At Arafat many of the pilgrims make their way to a small hill called Jabal Al Rahma, the Mountain of Mercy. It is where the Prophet Mohammed gave his last sermon in the year 632. The land rises only gently there but during this day of the pilgrimage, the dark brown granite hill is transformed into what looks like an enormous mound of sugar set in the desert. On every foothold along its slopes, on every boulder or stone large enough to stand on are the pilgrims, their *ihrams* painting the hill into a brilliant white.

It is here, where there are no grand buildings or mosques, a place surrounded only by the emptiness of the desert, that Muslims, clad in nothing more than a simple white robe, stand before Allah, and ask for absolution and forgiveness. It seems an odd place to want to be alone in the presence of one's God. At this loneliest of moments, amid the clamour of crowds of strangers, each person is trying to speak to God and unburden his or her soul of its innermost torments. People stand wherever they can find a space on the Mountain of Mercy, and with their hands cupped together, their palms turned towards the heavens in supplication, they beseech Allah, and offer up their prayers to Him. It is known as the 'Standing at Arafat'. People turn inwards to look at their lives, standing in the open desert where nothing can be hidden.

Gathered here are pilgrims from all over the world, from dozens of countries on all continents, of every skin colour, speaking a multitude of languages. Peasants from Pakistan and Afghanistan stand next to company directors and software engineers from Singapore or Britain. It is an experience that reveals the intensity and contradictions of the Hajj. You are among people with whom you have nothing in common except for a shared faith, and yet that faith alone is enough to give you a common identity. Pilgrims from poorer countries in Africa or South Asia travelling with the least means, often by bus or boat, can take a month to reach Mecca, while Muslims from western countries and the Gulf fly to Mecca and are greeted with the sort of comfort they are accustomed to. Yet in the performance of the rituals the Hajj is a place where your wealth, level of education, nationality and privileges become invisible. There are no reserved seating areas in any buildings, no faster routes along the way.

Many of my relatives have performed the Hajj: uncles and aunts, cousins near and distant, as well as relatives through my father's clan. However, even though it is incumbent on Muslims to perform the Hajj during their lifetime, for many the final decision to go ahead with the journey is often sparked by a particular event. The Quran says that when one performs the Hajj, one emerges like a newborn child into the world, cleansed of all sins and misdeeds. The Hajj is an opportunity to reflect and to begin again. My father told me that on that pilgrimage in 1972 he talked to three men on the eve of one of the main rituals of the pilgrimage. One man, my father said, was a Nigerian who had come to give thanks as his business had started to do well. Another man, a Palestinian, had come on the Hajj after his father had died, heartbroken, in exile in neighbouring Jordan, having fled there from his village in the West Bank which had been seized by Israel five years earlier in the Six Day War. The third man, from Sudan, had simply come to ask Allah to bless his family and allow them to prosper.

The Hajj is both a religious duty and a cultural need that reinforces for many Muslims the sense that, as Muslims, they are part of something beyond their nationality and race. It draws Muslims from all walks of life after the most harrowing experiences where lives and even countries have been destroyed. It is an undertaking that can provide a sense of belonging when all other things that give you stability have been shattered.

Even for such a diverse city as London there is something extraordinarily cosmopolitan about the borough of Ealing. When I was at university at the end of the 1980s, one of my friends lived there with his mother and his two siblings. It was a neat and affluent district but, like so many other parts of London, with enough public housing to make it feel like more than just a middle-class enclave. Twenty years later and the High Street is now a riotous mix of different cultures and races. It is home to a rising number of young eastern European émigrés, many of them Poles who work as cleaners or on London's building sites. There are Afghans, a large Indian and Pakistani neighbourhood, and one of the largest Somali communities in the country. The newer residents join Ealing's other long-established im-migrants, the Irish. On one side of the street is a cheap phone and internet café catering mainly to Poles, next door to it is the small Afghan restaurant that, unfortunately but predictably, is losing business to the fast food place across the road.

Just along from these two unlikely neighbours is a travel agency belonging to Mohammed Hassan. It seems indistinguishable from many of the other bucket shops on the High Street. Behind the deals posted up on neat cards in the front window there is a tidy, sparsely furnished reception area where four young men stare into their computer terminals and wedge telephones beneath their ears. A doorway at the back leads to Mohammed's office, a cramped box of a room with a wide desk overflowing with what seem to be audits and bank statements as well as a dusty computer and a telephone that never stops ringing. Every call rings on every phone at the same time. The office is run as a co-operative by Mohammed and his colleagues who have the gentle, serious looks of a group of students. Mohammed himself is a heavy-set man dressed, like his co-workers, in a suit but without a tie. And, like his colleagues, he has a beard.

Mohammed beckons me to sit down and begins to ask after my family. 'How's Mum and Dad? I hope they are both well and especially the Hajji [referring to my father by the honorific title of one who has made the pilgrimage to Mecca]. I hope his health is better.' He mentions my older sister Rakiya, whom he knows through her human rights reports during the war, and he asks how she is getting on now she is back home in Hargeisa.

I had never met Mohammed before that day and yet he knew exactly who I was and whom I was related to. Exile is a small world. When you meet a fellow Somali anywhere in the West you can usually find a connection – maybe you have met or worked with a relative of theirs in Canada or Saudi Arabia, or their father once had business dealings with yours in Somalia before the war, or their aunt in Dubai is married to a second cousin of your uncle. It is not so much an extended family as an extended society.

It is the month of Ramadan and I have arrived at Mohammed's offices just before noon prayers. 'Let us say our prayers before we start, Rageh,' he says. He points to a small door by the side of his desk, 'There is a small kitchen and bathroom in there, you can make your ablutions and then we'll go round the corner to the mosque.' He had already washed himself in preparation for prayers and so gave me directions to the mosque and headed out the back of his office. The washing before prayers is very precise. It isn't as simple as just washing your hands and feet. The process is called '*Wudu*' and there is a set order to the exercise. Before you start you declare your intention to pray in the name of Allah. Then, with clean water, you begin by washing your right hand up to the wrist followed by the left, both of them three times. Then you rinse your mouth out three times. You gently wash your nostrils three times. Then your face and ears, followed by forearms up to the elbows, then you pass a wet hand over your hair to the back of the neck, and you wash the backs of your ears and finally both feet. Only after you have completed this process in exactly that order, are you ready for prayer. I had not prayed at a mosque in over a year and, even though there was no one to see me in that tiny bathroom, I was a little nervous that I had forgotten the sequence. But as soon as the water touched my right hand it all came back to me.

The directions to the mosque were clear. Out of the office, second right, fifty or so yards down the alleyway. But I seemed to have made a mistake. The alleyway, overshadowed by dilapidated Victorian buildings stained black with the soot and smog from the high street's traffic, was empty. There was no mosque in sight. Then I heard footsteps and voices from the end of the alleyway. Two young North African men, both with thin, wispy beards, were heading up the High Street. They spotted me standing in the middle of the lane and when I greeted them in Arabic they responded. 'I'm looking for the Masjid,' I said.One of them pointed towards an old wooden door that seemed to be leading into someone's back garden. He pushed it open and waited for me to step inside.

Behind the creaking door I found a tiny patch of broken concrete which led into a passageway at the back of a Victorian building that looked as though it had once been a small warehouse. Shoes were scattered along the floor and crammed into wire-racks that had been bolted to the wall. The men were mostly in their twenties and I recognized the Somali and Sudanese among them immediately. The younger men, boys really, were Pakistani or Indian and wore white skullcaps and beige *shalwar kurtas*, the long, usually collarless, shirt and loose cotton trousers commonly worn by men in South Asia. The North Africans were fair with soft, loosely curling hair and the faint outline of a beard. I could hear the young men speaking in heavily accented Arabic as I drew closer. Just outside the prayer hall, in a small room where preachers would usually instruct groups of young men on the Quran or Islamic traditions, a tattered notice had been nailed to the wall: 'Any lessons or study groups which have not been author-ized by the imam or authorities are strictly not allowed. Please ask the mosque authorities if you wish to make study groups here and let them know who the teacher will be.'

This discreet building tucked away behind Ealing High Street is very different from the more famous London mosque, at Finsbury Park, which has been at the centre of so many news reports in recent years. Most non-Muslims would think of Finsbury Park Mosque as a back-street mosque where young men are radicalized. It isn't. It was built in 1990, at a cost of £8 million, and is an imposing redbrick building of four floors which serves around 20,000 local Muslims. It sits next door to the old Arsenal Football stadium in north London, its board of trustees is made up of well-known figures from the Muslim Association of Britain and, unlike the back-street mosque in Ealing, it is open to the public. In other words, it is a very accessible building with strong ties to the middle-class Muslim establishment in the capital. However, one man has come to define the mosque and the whole community as a dangerous and frightening place.

Abu Hamza al Masri, a radical Egyptian cleric who preached at Finsbury Park Mosque, who has lived in Britain for over twenty years and who has spoken openly of his support for militant causes, is probably the most widely, if not the only, recognizable Muslim cleric in the UK. In February 2006 he was convicted of crimes of racial hatred and incitement to murder and sentenced to seven years in prison. Since September 11 Abu Hamza al Masri appeared repeatedly in the media, representing, in its eyes, the angry Muslim radical, and representing, for most Muslims, a ludicrous, but also dangerous, caricature, so much so that long before 7th July many Muslim worshippers at Finsbury Park Mosque were so concerned about what he was saying that they complained to the police. The police did nothing. In 2003 the mosque authorities forbade him from preaching at the mosque. He was reduced to ranting and raving to a group of young men in the middle of the road in a street nearby. Of course, Abu Hamza al Masri is a media godsend, with his hook in place of a hand and his blind eye, but his appearances on television, isolated from the context of the rest of the British Muslim community, had very serious repercussions for the representation of Muslims in this country.

After his conviction the media proved him to be a conman with scant credentials as an imam, a fact which most of the local Muslims had been desperate to point out for some time. Unfortunately, it will take years before Finsbury Park Mosque ceases to be defined by Abu Hamza al Masri in the non-Muslim imagination. The mosque will continue to represent a sinister, secret, dangerous religion.

And yet here, in what *is* a back-street mosque hidden from view, invisible to non-Muslims, and carrying on an unreported existence, a small staff of wardens and preachers, like the imams at the grand, public mosque in Finsbury Park, watch over their modest property, careful to protect from wrong influences the young immigrants who flock here. Neither the public nor the more private place of worship is what it seems.

The mosque was full, even though it was noon prayers in the middle of a working day. Many of the young men had rushed out in their lunch hour from their shops and offices and as soon as the final prayers had been said they headed off back to work, leaving as quickly as they had come. Soon the prayer hall was silent and invisible once again.

Mohammed Hassan's travel agency specializes in two areas. They offer deals to British Somalis who want to return home to rediscover their roots, to introduce their British-born children to relatives and bring the family closer together. The other part of their business looks after British Somalis who want to make the Hajj pilgrimage to Mecca. In some ways, although they are very different journeys to very different places, the two sides of Mohammed's business fulfil the same need. They symbolize what lies at the heart of the British Muslim identity in modern Britain. It is a loyalty to three different worlds: a British nationality, a Somali heritage and the Islamic faith. If my father and mother were coming to Britain with me now and if we were making the journey back to Somalia via Mecca as we did more than thirty years ago we would use someone like Mohammed to help us on our way.

Just like my family, Mohammed never expected to settle permanently in Britain. As with me, it was education that brought him here. When the civil war ravaged Hargeisa, Mohammed fled into exile in Saudi Arabia. He was a young man, having finished his secondary education at the beginning of the 1980s. Like every other Somali boy he had been brought up with a Quranic education from pre-school age. The schools are known as 'Mal'amad' and children are taught to memorize the Quran and are instructed in its interpretation, as well as studying other subjects such as maths and science. This was the conventional way of educating your child, whatever your economic circumstances, and his, like mine, were comfortable. But the military dictatorship of General Siad Barre, like all secular dictatorships in the Islamic world, was obsessed with and paranoid about these young observant Muslim men, believing that mosques and Islamic societies were highly effective platforms for political organizations because they had local legitimacy and presence and a cultural authenticity that secular ideological slogans could never hope to attain. General Siad Barre's secret police began to fight an imagined enemy: they monitored mosques and preachers, and government members started to make aggressively secular speeches, associating all semblance of progress with the regime's ideology of 'scientific socialism'. In doing so, as we have seen so often before and since, they helped to create the very thing they believed they were fighting.

In July 1977 the Barre regime embarked on a disastrous war with Ethiopia over the Ogaden region, the area populated largely by Somalis but under the control of Ethiopia. The Barre dictatorship tried to present the conflict as a popular nationalist cause aimed at incorporating this Somali region of Ethiopia into a 'Greater Somalia', but it was a failure. Looking for a way out of the mess General Barre, having been an ally of the Soviet Union, switched sides overnight and began to court the West, requesting in particular military and economic aid from the United States.

Washington took the Siad Barre regime on as a Cold War client, in return for military bases that would give it access to the strategically important

Red Sea and Indian Ocean regions, which in turn provided southern access to the Arabian Peninsula from where a considerable amount of the West's oil supplies were transported via the Red Sea and up through the Suez Canal. As the Ogaden war started to turn against Siad Barre, he embarked on a domestic campaign against those whom he imagined would take advantage of his failed military adventure abroad. The attacks against Muslim groups began in earnest in 1978 with the outlawing of the wearing of the *hejab* and the banning of Muslim societies. The aim was to wipe out the public face of Islam and to force it to become a private, hidden religion.

'I remember the student protests in 1979,' Mohammed says, 'when I became involved in the movement against the dictatorship. The government made it compulsory for young girls to wear short-sleeve shirts! Can you imagine?' It was a policy that was not perceived simply as an attack on Islamic groups by Somali society, but in effect as a wholesale attack on a Muslim society which at that time had conservative values, particularly when it came to sexual mores. Male and female students protested, and their parents supported them. It was a period of political awakening for Mohammed and many other young men of his generation. But the politicization of the young in northern Somalia did not mean that they simply joined 'Islamist' opposition. The opposition against the Siad Barre dictatorship grew into a national campaign for human rights, of which Islamic values were a part. The Somali National Movement, which was to become the primary political and military rebel movement instrumental in destroying Siad Barre's control of northern Somalia, was a patchwork of different voices which came together to get rid of a hated military junta. Opposition to Barre included members of Islamic groups such as the Muslim Brotherhood, as well as prominent religious leaders, a multitude of clan elders, academics and businessmen. None of these groups had a purely Islamic agenda, but equally none of them would have had the same kind of national legitimacy had they been purely secular in their ideology and outlook.

Mohammed was picked up during the student protests in the many random large-scale regular secret police operations against the imagined enemy that had now become very real. Thousands were rounded up often for no other reason than that they 'looked the type'. Mohammed smiles wryly. 'There are aspects of what happened then that are similar with what's happening here today. No one is being randomly picked up and being locked away without charge for ages,' he pauses, then adds with a darkly sarcastic laugh, 'at least not yet. But what is more familiar is this belief that you can defeat young Islamists by banning mosques and imams that just look or sound like they are trouble. I can tell the West, from first-hand experience, this not only doesn't work, it helps to confirm and harden these young men in their beliefs.'

He leans back in his chair. 'When I was taken to the police station in Hargeisa after the student demonstrations, I was taken there on suspicion – they had no evidence against me. I went in simply as a young student who, like all the other students, was Muslim. I knew little about real political organization and opposition, few of us did. But after the weeks we were kept in that prison we all came out as different men, with a bond, a sense of unified purpose and commitment. The security services and police rounded us up so they could prevent us from using the mosque, either as a place of worship or identity or political organization, but we just brought the mosque into our prison cells.' Mohammed describes how all of them began to pray together in the cells and those who were initially more afraid of what was happening found strength. 'There were other prisoners, who'd been brought there before us but for different reasons. Some of them had become "secular Muslims" if you like, they didn't pray much any more and so on, but, like us, they were opposed to the regime. They became inspired and motivated by our example.'

Mohammed returns to the subject of life in Britain these days. 'I wish I could tell them, these commentators who attack British imams and the Ulema wholesale in this country that these men are part of the solution and you don't even realize it. Who will talk to these radicalized young men? The commentators in newspapers? The television journalists and policemen? Is that who they think these young men will be prepared to listen to? Whether you like them or not, whether you are suspicious of them or not, it is the imams in the small local mosques, *not* those few big names who meet government ministers or go on television, who can have the authority and legitimacy to guide and educate these young men away from the path of violence and terrorism. But these commentators just don't seem to want to hear that.'

After being released Mohammed knew that there was no future for him in northern Somalia while it was misruled by the Siad Barre regime. He went to work in Saudi Arabia, as tens of thousands of Somalis and Sudanese did. They would send money home to their families every month and their remittances from their jobs as porters, cleaners and attendants was, and still is, a critical element in sustaining the economies of their home countries. By the end of the 1980s, as the civil war in Somalia had reached its most ferocious stage in the north of the country, Mohammed made a life-changing decision. 'As you know, all our families knew that the regime was facing certain defeat in the end. I wanted to be ready for that moment, to have something to offer in rebuilding the country.' He applied for a student visa to study in Britain. He could support himself from the money he had earned in Saudi Arabia. He applied to study biochemistry and in October 1990 took up a place at the University of Surrey. 'For people of my parents' generation, the sciences, especially medical sciences, had a particular cachet. It was not just because medicine was a respected or lucrative profession that set it apart. Most of my parents' generation would have first come across white people working as doctors and nurses in their local village or town. For them, the ability to heal the sick and the elderly was overwhelmingly identified with white people who came to the developing world as missionaries and volunteers. To a large extent this is still the case today even though there are now many more African doctors and nurses working alongside white NGOs. In the minds of older Somalis scientific knowledge meant advanced

Western knowledge and so a doctor who was black, African and Muslim was so much more impressive than a black Muslim lawyer or accountant.

'I chose it because biochemists are essential,' Mohammed says. 'Doctors need the findings of biochemists in order to be able to distinguish between different illnesses as many symptoms often appear to be the same.' In his choice, Mohammed was also becoming an unlikely pioneer: 'I still remember so clearly one of the things I wrote in my application form to the University of Surrey in 1989. I wrote down that at the time of applying there wasn't a single biochemist in Somalia who had qualified to the level of post-graduate university degree.'

A few months after Mohammed began his course, in January 1991, the Siad Barre regime collapsed. The dictator and what remained of the forces loyal to him temporarily based themselves in the south-west of the country, from where they tried to launch a counter-offensive to take the capital of Mogadishu from rival clan-based rebel groups. But the civil war which had begun in the north in 1988 was now unstoppable and quickly spread to the rest of the country, where all central authority or control had disappeared and any effective military power was scattered between rival warlords. In 1991 the north declared independence from the rest of Somalia,

calling itself the Republic of Somaliland, and remained largely stable and peaceful. But in the rest of
Somalia, the implosion of the central state and the
influx into Mogadishu of rival and heavily armed
clan-based militia signalled the start of the long and
catastrophic destruction of the country, a situation
that remains to this day.

The United States had stayed loyal to Siad Barre
to the very end. It was essentially an amoral alliance
in which Washington remained entirely uninterested
in the regime's human rights abuses, as long as the
US had access to military bases and assets in the
country. Somalia was sold large amounts of military
equipment and, in return, it exported bananas and
citrus fruit to the West. However, aid importation,
from the US in particular, weaned Somalia on to
reliance on imported foodstuffs. Indigenous agriculture was eroded and so, by the time the civil war
broke out, the conditions had been set for Somalia
to be unable to withstand conflict and drought. The
two combined, and together with the militias fighting for control over scarce food resources, made the
onset of famine inevitable. Somalia as a nation-state
had been undone.

Having come to Britain on a recognized passport,
Mohammed found himself suddenly stateless. 'I had
begun the course as probably one of the wealthiest

students. I had around £5,000 with me from my work in Saudi Arabia, but by the time the course ended in 1992 I was probably the poorest person on the course,' he said, shaking his head. One day you have a passport from a recognized country: Somalia, Liberia, Sierra Leone, Afghanistan, Iraq. The next moment you are a stateless person, with no work and no prospects. 'My biggest concern during those days,' Mohammed says, and at this stage, speaking in Somali, he uses a colloquial aphorism, 'was to find something that would enable me to walk.' This line comes from Somalia's nomad tradition. Being unable to walk in this context does not mean a literal physical disability; it means you are unable to roam freely. As Somali society became increasingly urbanized in the latter part of the twentieth century, the phrase came to mean an inability to travel into town to get to market and trade, or to buy goods or simply to meet friends.

'It was a really, really hard situation for someone who had grown up to be independent.' What cut most deeply was the sense of waste and the terrible guilt that came with it. 'Twenty years of education had come to nothing.' He did not mean that he had wasted so many years in education only to find that he could not obtain work that was relevant to his training. He was talking of his feelings of guilt about the sacrifices that his family had had to make in order for him to have an education, and that those sacrifices seemed to have been for nothing.

As he talked, Mohammed began to write figures on the notepad on his desk. 'From the time I finished my secondary education in Hargeisa at the beginning of the 1980s, let's just say, from 1979, until the start of my degree at Surrey, that's 1990,' he wrote the dates out, 'that's eleven years study at my parents' expense. I was the person they put all their dreams into. That money came from other sources: other relatives who would not get as good or as long an education as me, others who would have to live at home longer because they could not be given the means to start up on their own.' He paused for a moment, still gazing down at the numbers on his pad. 'Calculated another way, I basically lost a quarter of my life. Imagine if I had spent those thirteen years working as a porter or a labourer somewhere. I would have been able to provide something for my family, or at least they would not have had to go through as much hardship, and maybe I would not have been in the predicament that I was. I thought I was obtaining an education that would be of benefit to so many people: my family, even my country. I ended up learning the wrong thing at exactly the wrong time. I began to meet other

Somali health professionals, who, like me, had come to Britain to get an education and were now stranded. There were about thirty of them: doctors, dentists and health technicians, who were all unemployed because they were overqualified for the kind of work we suddenly needed in order to survive.'

Mohammed had drifted in and out of many jobs when he decided in July 1992 to go to Bristol, where there was a tiny but long-settled Somali community dating back to the beginning of the century. At that time there were about forty Somalis living there; today there are between six and seven thousand. He continued to flit from job to job while he tried to find a business of his own. In 1994 he made a trip to Saudi Arabia to see if it was worth emigrating back there but, disillusioned, he returned to Britain.

The early years of the 1990s saw the biggest and most sustained settlement of Somali refugees in the UK. As the civil war destroyed Mogadishu and the rest of Somalia, Somali communities grew apace across British cities: London, Bristol, Sheffield, Liverpool, Manchester, Cardiff and Leicester. Mohammed became one of the first Somalis to start a business to serve this expanding community. Most of their needs were the concerns of all newly exiled communities: how to make contact with relatives who had been dispersed to other countries or who had become stranded in neighbouring countries and refugee camps and how to send them money. For a refugee, or for that matter for anyone who is poor in Britain, it is difficult and expensive to have a telephone line installed or to open a bank account. To send money through a money transfer bureau, or to make an international phone call in a booth on the high street is easier and quicker and all you need is a bit of cash. Telecom shops and money-transfer businesses in corner shops and at the back of local cafés have grown across British cities over the last ten years. Mohammed opened a money-transfer shop in Bristol and the business gave him back his self-confidence. However, by 2000 he had married and had had children and his business was still a transitory, hand-to-mouth affair that did not provide enough to support his new family in an expensive city.

That year he moved from Bristol to London, where there was a much larger Somali community, then numbering about 50,000. Today the figure is around 70,000. It had been seven years since the most terrible days of the war and famine when the largest numbers of people were forced to flee into exile. In those seven years, many thousands had come to join other family members to settle in Britain as refugees from war and persecution, and during that time many Somalis who had arrived earlier made the transition from being asylum seekers and refugees to being British citizens. Like Mohammed, they started families and soon there was a generation of Somalis born as Britons in Britain.

Until Somalis became British citizens it had been almost impossible to perform the Hajj, or indeed to leave Britain at all, because Somali passports were no longer recognized as there was no central government, and it was not possible to travel on refugee documents. 'When we decided to start our travel agency, we did so with a clear view of the market opportunity,' Mohammed said. 'Firstly, Somalis were beginning to settle here and take up citizenship, which meant they were once again able to travel, and because they had held on to their identities as Muslims *and* Somalis they needed to travel to the Hajj and also back to visit family in Somalia.' His idea made complete sense, culturally and commercially. It was an unexpected turning point in Mohammed's life. 'Throughout my life, from the day I went to the Mal'amad until now, I have always stayed with the mosque. I have never deserted it. But I never imagined I'd go into this kind of business after settling here. I thought that if I was lucky it would be something in the medical field or maybe a corner shop.'

The travel agency sells about 6,000 tickets a year. The vast majority are for Somalis returning, especially to the self-declared Republic of Somaliland in the north of the country, which is largely stable and secure. Most of the tickets are sold for travel in the summer months and the school holidays. 'If you'd come to talk to me in May,' Mohammed says, laughing, 'we'd have no place to sit, and no time to discuss anything. The place is packed, the phones are ringing off the hook. It's quite a scene.'

It is believed that about 20,000 British Somalis return to the capital of Somaliland, Hergeisa, every year between the months of July and August. Tens of thousands more come from other European countries with sizeable Somali populations: principally Holland, Denmark, Norway and Sweden. Thousands of others also arrive from the United States and Canada. Most Somalis living in the West can afford only one foreign trip or holiday a year and so for many the priority is to be able to return to Somalia. When they travel they carry gifts and essentials that their relatives cannot buy at home: particularly clothes or medicines, or hard-to-find medical equipment for elderly relatives, toys for children, or simply money. Whoever you are and whatever your status, it's unimaginable to return to Somalia without a lot of luggage. In part the gifts are a way of reassuring relatives that life for those in their families who have settled in the West has indeed been good. It helps to delay momentarily the worries over housing, education and lack of employment. But it is also about giving something to those relatives who have remained behind and whose access to basic goods and minor luxuries is far more limited.

Making this journey back to Somalia is a financially daunting undertaking for a community that is still largely economically marginalized in the UK. 'The average size of family which returns each summer is about five,' says Mohammed, turning to his jotting pad once again to write down the figures as he makes his point. 'Each ticket is about £400, then there are all the gifts and money that you have to take back to relatives. There is little cost once you get there as most people stay with relatives, although a few do go to the hotels that are springing up in Hargeisa and other major towns. But as you know from having been back there, you have to entertain and see *a lot* of relatives whom you haven't seen for a long time: cousins, uncles, aunts, you name it. So it's an expensive thing. But it is essential. With our roots, we have to do it. We would not be who we are,' he points at me emphatically, 'if we didn't do it.'

The Hajj, and what it represents, is also a part of

this same identity. 'The Hajj is a religious duty, but simple economics has made it a luxury for British Somalis,' Mohammed says. 'Our economic situation is different from other British Muslims, like British Arabs or Asians. The average price of a Hajj tour is between £2,500 and £3,000. That's out of the price range for Somalis who, if they can afford a trip in a year, will take their family to Somalia.' About 27,000 British Muslims go to Mecca for the Hajj every year. The vast majority are British Asians from Pakistan and India. 'Somalis don't go on the same tours as British Asians because they are too expensive. They want the cheapest possible flights and accommodation. They don't want to go Emirates or BA, or stay in three- or four-star accommodation.' So Mohammed and his colleagues invented what they call a 'supersaver ticket' for the Hajj, at around £1,300. It includes flights, all accommodation and transfers. It soon began to attract pilgrims from other communities who were similarly economically disadvantaged.

'Afghans, Yemenis and other Africans use our services now as well.' Mohammed shrugs his shoulders and what could be mistaken for a pang of regret flashes across his face. 'We don't cater for Arabs, Pakistanis or British converts to Islam and the reason for that is simply economics – they travel in a completely different way from our Somali community. The free market has got in the way, and it's a shame because one of the defining things about the Hajj, of course, is that when you get there, the central spiritual and religious purpose of the place is that it is mixed: there are no classes, no races, men and women perform the pilgrimage together. I'd love to be able to reflect that in my business. But in getting to Mecca now as western Muslims, we are divided by the amount of money in our pocket. That's part of what being in the West is about, I suppose.'

But Mohammed remembered one time when he did take on the Hajj a group of British Muslims who were drawn from more than just the Somali community. 'In 2002 I took a very mixed group, and it was GREAT! The Hajj is always a remarkable and wonderful experience, but this particular journey to Mecca made it even more so. Back home in the UK when you get such a diverse group of Muslims together, we have our Islamic identities in common, for sure, and that is very important, but there is so much which is different about us: our cultural habits, how we talk. Somalis have quite a brutal and direct sense of humour and are quite argumentative which is maybe different from how Afghans are used to dealing with things, which in turn might annoy some Yemenis. But in Mecca what was amazing was that all those things that I thought would be there, were not. All this stuff that commentators refer to as multiculturalism, I don't know what they mean by it, they don't explain it to people like me although it is people like me it affects most directly. All I know is that what I witnessed on that trip is what binds us as British Muslims. Maybe it was because it was the first Hajj after nine eleven? I don't know. But all of us, with our different races, from different continents with different languages, we were brothers and sisters.'

In such a fractured and largely secular world, the idea of a global religious community which despite huge linguistic, racial and cultural differences among its followers still feels a sense of unity can seem fanciful and idealistic. But outside a mosque in Nigeria I have seen people collecting money for a Palestinian charity. After prayers at a mosque in Sweden I saw collections for people in Chechen and outside British mosques across the country there have been collections for earthquake victims in Iran and Afghanistan as well as for more overtly political campaigns and causes from Iraq to Uzbekistan. What binds them? What makes everyday working Muslims leaving Friday prayers the length and breadth of Britain, as well as those Muslims who haven't prayed or been to the mosque in years, feel a commitment to Muslims in these lands which many British Muslims have never seen?

The story of my parents' pilgrimage thirty years ago and the story of Mohammed, who in a sense has refound himself and a purpose in life through the Hajj, demonstrates that perhaps the things we share as British Muslims are much stronger than the things that divide us.

4. The Catastrophic War

Shortly before Christmas 2005, just after Ramadan, British television news was dominated for one night by the deaths of three Britons. They had been killed while travelling north on the road from Najaf to Baghdad. They were not western contractors kidnapped by extremists; they were not soldiers serving with British forces in southern Iraq and they were not journalists. Their names were Yahya Gulamali, Husain Mohammedali and Saifuddin Makai. Mr Makai and Mr Mohammedali had been lifelong friends. They owned successful businesses in London, both had young children, and they belonged to the same mosque, the Hussaini mosque in Northolt. These were family men, by all accounts content in their identities as British Muslims. They were on a pilgrimage.

Gulamali, Mohammedali and Makai were travelling by bus back to Baghdad after visiting the shrines of Najaf, Karbala and Kufa. The road north to Baghdad from the relatively safer southern regions of Iraq passes through two of the capital's suburbs, Mahmoudiya and Latifiyah, which are almost completely controlled by Al Qaeda-linked groups. These neighbourhoods are strongholds of the most fanatical of extremists, whose aim is to induce sectarian hatred. They are very dangerous places. Buses carrying Shia pilgrims along the main trunk road south to Najaf and Karbala through these districts are welcome soft targets, and the one carrying these Britons was no exception. The three men shared the bus with many other Shia Muslim pilgrims from around the world – from Britain, as well as India and South Africa. Two other British pilgrims were wounded in the attack.

The grieving families of Mr Mohammedali and Mr Makai, supported by the Hussaini mosque, had to decide what to do with the corpses of their loved ones. Under Muslim custom the dead have to buried as quickly as possible. The relatives in England expressed the wish that the men, the heads of their families, be buried in a Shia cemetery close to the holy shrines which they had been visiting. In the end they were buried near the shrine of Imam Hussain in Karbala, after whom their mosque in west London was named.

The news of their deaths seemed to come and go in a flash. It seemed no more tragic or remarkable than the reports of more Iraq deaths that week, or of Westerners kidnapped or soldiers killed and wounded. But the men's presence in Iraq *was* significant. These were law-abiding, middle-aged, professional British Muslims on a bus pilgrimage in one of the most violent places in the world. Was this story not worthy of closer examination?

Every year, amid the car bombs and tank fire, at least 5,000 British Muslims go on pilgrimages to Iraq, and yet we are all much more aware of the small number of European Muslims going there to fight. At the time of writing, there are only four documented cases of European militants in Iraq: one Dutch, one Belgian and two French, although there are probably a handful more, perhaps thirty at most.

In polls conducted by ICM and other organizations after the London attacks, it was claimed that the majority of people in Britain believed that their country's involvement in the war in Iraq was directly connected to the rise in terrorism in the UK. But why Iraq? What is it about Iraq which has made it such a compelling cause for young *jihadis* from all over the world? Is it because the lawlessness and chaos of Iraq today provide a useful base for groups linked to the Al Qaeda network? Well, why not Afghanistan? There are far fewer US and British troops there than in Iraq, the central government has no effective power of its own and relies on the co-operation of brutal warlords who are hated and feared by the majority of Afghans. Furthermore the tribal areas of Waziristan between Afghanistan and Pakistan where Osama Bin Laden is believed to be hiding are a safe haven for them. Are they drawn to Iraq because it is just another failed state where they can operate? Why does my own country, Somalia, where there is no government, no UN, no international presence whatsoever cause such little consternation? And what compels 5,000 British Muslims to risk their lives in a war zone to visit the holy shrines in Iraq?

If Mecca and Medina are the places where the principles of the Islamic religion were born, Baghdad is where Arab and Islamic civilizations flourished. Iraq is where the heritage of all Muslims lies, not just in an historical sense, but as a living symbol of Islamic identity.

By 632, the year in which he died, the Prophet Mohammed had succeeded in doing what no other person or group had done in Arabia: he had managed to unite the major tribes of the peninsula under a new religion and identity – Islam. Families and clans whose individual and collective loyalties had been to their tribes, now saw themselves as being part of a religious and ideological community that was greater than their blood allegiances. By doing this, the Prophet Mohammed had brought a new level of peace and security to the communities of the Arabian Peninsula. In the wake of his death, the task of spreading the message of Islam while at the same time building and governing this growing community of believers, the *Ummah*, fell to the Prophet Mohammed's closest followers and companions. However, the Prophet's was a divinely inspired mission, as the Messenger of God, while his followers, in contrast, had to rely on instinct.

As Islam began to spread beyond the desert confines of the peninsula, the first Caliphs, the Rashidun (the Rightly Guided Ones), who had come from the Prophet's innermost circle, started shaping the way in which the rapidly growing Islamic community would be governed: a single community with a single leader. Only five years after the Prophet's death, the Arabs of the peninsula, under the second Caliph, Umar, took the newly established religion of Islam beyond the desert for the first time, into Iraq, then Syria and Egypt. The battle of Qadissiyah in Iraq in 637 led to the fall of the Persian Sassanid Empire that had previously ruled Mesopotamia, as Iraq was then known.

The capital of the Persian Empire in Iraq was at Ctesiphon, about twenty-five miles south-east of Baghdad. The only visible remnant of the city that fell to the Arabs is the magnificent second-century Arch of Ctesiphon, which was the grand entrance to the principal audience hall of the Sassanid emperors and now straddles one of the main arterial roads into the south-eastern approaches to the Iraqi capital.

Two days before the invasion of Iraq in 2003 I went to look at the Arch of Ctesiphon. It was a breathtaking sight. The vast vaulted archway made entirely of baked bricks that shone golden brown in the afternoon light rose majestically from the flat landscape almost ninety feet into the sharp blue sky. It was flanked on either side by the decaying walls of the old palace, its delicate arches carved into the sandy brickwork. The Arch of Ctesiphon marks the beginning of Islam's flowering in the Middle East. Within a year of the battle of Qadissiyah and the defeat of the Persian Sassanids, Jerusalem was conquered, then Palestine, North Africa and Persia.

In 656 the expanding Islamic Empire under the

Caliphate experienced what many other expanding empires have faced: a mutiny by discontented commanders. The last of the Rashidun Caliphs, Uthman, was assassinated by commanders who felt aggrieved that they were not being allowed to benefit enough from their conquests. They proclaimed Ali, who like Uthman was a son-in-law of the Prophet, their new Caliph. It was the beginning of the first civil war in Islam, the first division within Islam, or '*Fitna*', as it is called. The rebels, led by Ali, marched to Basra where most of their supporters had gathered. There Ali found himself in a terrible dilemma: on the one hand he could not abandon his partisans, yet neither could he condone the murder of Uthman who was, after all, a relative of the Prophet and had been killed inside his own home in Medina. Ali and his partisans were based in the city of Kufa, five miles north of Najaf. One of the first things he had to do on arrival was put down a rebellion in Basra, which had been backed by members of the prominent families of Mecca, including Aisha, the widow of the Prophet, who saw Ali's claim to the Caliphate as illegitimate. The uprising against Ali was defeated in Basra, in the Battle of the Camel. One of the rebel leaders, Az Zubayr, who had been a prominent companion of the Prophet, was killed.

The town bearing his name, Zubayr, stands on

the border between present–day Iraq and Kuwait, and was one of the first cities to be captured by invading British forces in 2003. Today it still has a large Sunni population and is one of the few places in southern Iraq where there is support for Sunni insurgency groups. Ali's forces came to be known as 'Shi' at al-Ali', those who follow Ali. It was directly from this lineage that the Shia tradition of Islam was born in the following few years.

As the lands controlled by their forces expanded, the Ummayad family, who were Uthman's kinsmen, established their formal capital in Damascus. Faced with what they saw as a usurper, they had to avenge not just Uthman's murder but also the open challenge to their Caliphate. They were supported in this by the wealthy tribes and principal families of Mecca. As fighting between the forces continued, the unchecked bloodshed among the closest relatives and companions of the Prophet was becoming too damaging and its potential consequences for the balance of power in the area too dangerous for it to be allowed to continue much longer. In 657 neutral Muslim leaders assembled near the Euphrates river to arbitrate in the conflict. They did not succeed. Ali was accused by a radical group of his partisans, known as the 'Kharajites', or secessionists, of bowing to the claims on the Caliphate by the Ummayad family. Then they murdered him. But in the stronghold of Kufa, just outside Najaf, backing for Ali's cause did not diminish, and his supporters called on Ali's second son, Hussain.

Hussain was the grandson of the Prophet Mohammed, and there are several references in early Islamic scriptures to the Prophet's deep love for him. The 'Hadith A'Kissa', the Hadith of the Cloak, describes how Hussain and his older brother, Hassan, were part of the House of the Prophet, and how the Prophet had rushed to see his two grandsons as soon as news of their birth reached him.

Hussain, his family, his followers and their wives and children made their way in a caravan towards Kufa. They were met by the overwhelming forces of the Ummayads on the plains of Karbala, just outside Najaf. In the battle that ensued, every single member of Hussain's entourage – men, women and children – was slaughtered. The Ummayad forces allowed him to live until the end of the massacre. When Hussain asked for water for his six-month-old son who lay dying in his arms, legend has it that the enemy shot a poisoned arrow at the neck of the child, to 'quench his thirst'. Hussain was then killed and decapitated.

For Shia Muslims Hussain's death symbolizes the nature of injustice and how it is passed from one generation to another, and reinforces the Shia's sense of being a persecuted minority. However, the veneration of Hussain and Ali within Islam is not exclusive to the Shia tradition. Hussain is also known across Islam, in both Sunni and Shia traditions, as 'Sayyid al-Shuhad', the Leader of Martyrs. His father, Ali, the founder of the Shia tradition, is accorded an even greater level of respect, regardless of tradition or sect. He is known by all Muslims as 'Emir Al Mu'miniin', the Commander of the Faithful, and the Prophet Mohammed called him 'Abu Turab', the Father of the Soil. As a cousin and son-in-law of the Messenger of God, Ali is regarded by Sunnis as one of the first people on earth to convert to Islam. As a member of the Prophet's household he is held up as the last of the Rashidun, the first four 'rightly guided' Caliphs of Islam. He is believed to be buried in Najaf in the magnificent gold tomb of Imam Ali.

During the six years I spent reporting from Iraq I visited the shrine many times, when the country was ruled by Saddam Hussain and since it has been under US and British occupation. The mausoleum of Imam Ali lies at the heart of Najaf city. Across the road from the gates of the shrine are the crowded, narrow streets and alleyways of the old covered market. The busiest shops and stalls immediately surround the compound. Nowadays all around you can hear voices from America and Britain, and you see many families who have travelled from Iran to visit and pray at the mosque. Each year thousands of Shia pilgrims flock towards the great wooden and copper gates of the mausoleum. On entering the shrine you emerge into a dazzling white marble courtyard, about 100 yards long on each of its four sides. Arches line the outer walls of the courtyard, leading into the administrative offices, storerooms and teaching halls of the religious authorities. The friezes along the top of the high wall and each arch are inlaid with a mosaic of tiny tiles of a blue that matches the sky overhead, and a bright turquoise and rusted brown. Rising from the centre of the brilliant white marble floor are the tomb and mosque. The dome is painted in shimmering, glittering gold leaf and on either side of the structure stand two minarets, also entirely covered in gold leaf. A cavernous alcove with its high ceiling leads you into the prayer hall and the tomb of Imam Ali.

Najaf is also home to an academy known as the 'Hawza Ilmiya', and is the most prestigious seat of instruction for Shia clerics and Ayatollahs in the world. There are other 'Hawza' academies, in the Iranian holy city of Qom and in London, but neither has Najaf's historical authority and legitimacy. Grand Ayatollah Ali al Sistani, the spiritual leader of Iraq's majority Shia Muslims and thus the most influential, if not the most powerful, man in Iraq, was taught there. Najaf was also the home in exile of another Ayatollah, one who reshaped the nature of political Islam in the modern world: Khomeini. In 1965 the future leader of the Islamic Revolution in Iran settled in Najaf. He was to spend the next thirteen years there, teaching classes and instructing young clerics from all over the Shia world. It was while in Najaf that Khomeini developed what remain probably the most controversial key theories within political Islam: a concept of Islamic governance that argues that clerics should not be confined simply to religion, but that they must govern and take charge of the political process.

Najaf is symbolic even in death. Beyond the shrine lies Wadi A'Salaam, the Valley of Peace. It is a small town, only about four square miles, with clearly marked roads and narrow passageways for pedestrians. However, none but the dead reside in the Valley of Peace, about 5 million of them, including many senior religious figures and clerics. It is the largest cemetery in the world. I have attended Friday prayers inside the shrine on several occasions and watched many families bear their deceased relatives inside the simplest of coffins made of rough planks of wood hastily nailed together. Huge crowds attend the shrine on Fridays and so the coffins are borne high above the shoulders of the worshippers as people clear a path for the grieving family. The coffin is first taken inside the mausoleum to bring the deceased close to the tomb of Imam Ali before burial. After a few minutes the family carries the coffin out of the shrine and walks down the short path to the Valley of Peace. Shia Muslims believe that to be buried here is not simply a special honour, but is the first step to being granted entry into heaven. These days the cemetery is so overcrowded that many people are now buried standing up.

Close to Najaf is the city of Karbala, scene of the martyrdom of Hussain in 680. Hussain is buried in the town, and both the road from Baghdad to the north-east and the road from Najaf immediately to the south lead to the centre of the city where his shrine is located. The shrine occupies two separate compounds about 300 yards apart, separated by a promenade lined with palm tress. The main one houses the mosque with its dome of gold leaf and minarets, where Hussain's body lies. The second compound, built and decorated in similar fashion, is the shrine to Hussain's half-brother, Abbas, who was also killed at Karbala. In many ways, Karbala is of greater significance in the global political climate today than Najaf, because no other religious place in the Islamic world is as synonymous with the concept of martyrdom. Before the battle in which Hussain was killed by Ummayad forces Karbala was uninhabited; the city exists as a direct result of what happened to Hussain and his followers. But Karbala is not there simply to commemorate Imam Hussain as the grandson of the Prophet Mohammed, it is much more about remembering the unjust nature of his death, the way in which he and his relatives were killed by far more powerful forces than his own.

The day of Hussain's martyrdom is commemorated every year across the Muslim world in the Festival Ashoura, which takes place on the tenth day of the month of Muharram in the Islamic calendar. In some countries the men flail their backs with metal chains. In others, such as Lebanon, incisions are made with razor blades in the scalps of every Shia male, from young boys to elderly men, who then march through the streets, beating their bleeding heads, to signify the beheading of Hussain.

The nearby city of Kufa, which, like Najaf and Karbala, lies on the banks of the Euphrates, is also a deeply significant site. And there is Ur, which today lies just outside the city of Nassiriyah, and which, according to the Old Testament, is the birthplace of

Abraham. For most Muslims, towns such as Najaf or Ur are as familiar as Bethlehem is to people brought up in a Christian environment.

In August 2004 I heard news of an imminent US offensive against impoverished, urban followers of the young, ambitious and aggressive Shia cleric Moqtada al Sadr. Throughout the spring of that year, al Sadr had antagonized American forces and the US-led occupation authorities in Iraq. He had used all political, propaganda and military tools at his disposal in this effort, aimed ultimately at creating a large populist appeal for himself among ordinary Iraqis. Paul Bremer, the then US administrator in Iraq and head of the US-led occupying body, made the decision to confront al Sadr and his forces who had based themselves in Najaf. From the outset of his installation as effectively Washington's proconsul in Iraq, Mr Bremer seemed to make up policy as he went along. On 5 April he declared Moqtada al Sadr 'an outlaw'. The Shia cleric decided to retreat to Najaf, presuming that America was aware of the city's symbolic importance to Muslims around the world and its role as a centre of Islamic study and pilgrimage and thus would never contemplate an assault on the city. (The last person to launch a military attack on Najaf had been Saddam Hussein in the wake of the first Gulf War, in response to the uprising against his rule by Shias in the south and Kurds in the north.) Moqtada al Sadr wanted to make the connection to Imam Ali in the minds of the Muslim public both inside and outside Iraq: that he too faced a stronger enemy in an unjust battle. The stand-off could not have been more full of cultural and historical references. Moqtada al Sadr made sure of it. But US and British forces did not see it this way, nor did the foreign media to a large extent. Many of the major British and American news organizations had correspondents reporting from Najaf and even from inside Imam Ali's shrine during the attack.

The assault started at the beginning of August. For the briefest of moments the journalist in me paid attention to the strategy of the conflict: how long would the attack last and how many people would be killed? What would this do to Moqtada al Sadr's political aspirations? Having briefly stood up to the Americans would he rejoin the political process in Iraq? How would his involvement affect the over-whelmingly Shia south which is the British army's sector of operations? This train of thought lasted no more than half a minute. Then an American helicopter gunship that had been hovering over the centre of the city fired a missile. Thick black columns of smoke rose from several parts of the city, and there in the middle of the frame were the gold dome and minarets of Imam Ali's shrine. I raised my hand to my forehead and shouted in a voice that seemed to come out of me by itself, 'Oh my God! Imam Ali. Fuck! I don't believe it!' Then, for a few minutes, I could not speak.

The battle lasted three weeks. Najaf was attacked with artillery, tanks and helicopter gunships. US forces fought in the streets around the Imam Ali shrine with armoured personnel carriers loaded with heavy machine guns and mortar launchers. Moqtada al Sadr's overwhelmed militia, hopelessly out-numbered by several thousand US Marines and Iraqi army troops in support, hid in the shrine and in the thousands of paths and alleys that wove in and out of the millions of graves in the Valley of Peace. At the end of the three weeks much of the centre of Najaf lay in ruins. Karl Vick, an American reporter who was attached to the Marines during their assault on the city, stood amid the destruction and discussed the scene with the US commanders in charge of the mission: 'The gold-domed Imam Ali shrine re-mained all but unscathed,' the correspondent wrote in an article entitled 'Iraqi Holy City Left Broken by Urban Warfare' in the *Washington Post* of 27 August 2004, but the core of the city around it, a destination of longing for millions of Shiite Muslims, is so mauled that American commanders debate which famously ruined wartime cityscape Najaf now resembles most.

'It's like Stalingrad,' a senior 5th Cavalry officer said.

'Sarajevo,' Marine Lt-Col. Rainey maintained.

'Beirut,' a Marine commander said.

'Not Dresden,' an army field officer said while standing watch at a panorama of blackened, half-destroyed buildings a few dozen yards north of the glittering shrine. 'Not enough fire.'

Hundreds of militiamen had been killed, as well as civilians, and considerable parts of the Valley of Peace cemetery had been completely destroyed. In their actions, Moqtada al Sadr and his followers demonstrated contempt for the people of Najaf. Their own political interests were the only thing that mattered in their confrontation with US forces and the installed interim Iraqi government. But was he worth it? Was limiting his political support worth the decimation of this holy city?

Details of the fighting continued to be reported but interest in the significance of the attack dwindled except in Muslim communities. There were riots and protests across Iraq, from Basra to Mosul. In Fallujah, one of the most vehemently Sunni Ba'athist towns in the country, 3,000 civilians protested against the assault.

The reaction of one man whom few people in the West had heard of then, or now, encapsulated just how this episode in the war was seen by the Muslim and Arab world. Mohammed Bahr al Uloum is a senior Shia cleric. He was a long-time ardent opponent of Saddam Hussein and, like so many Shia clerics, lost many members of his family to the regime and was forced into exile. After the invasion of Iraq, despite scepticism of America's motives in Iraq, he decided to join in the country's multi-ethnic transitional bodies. He was President of Iraq's Governing Council, the country's interim government until full elections took place. If there was one Shia cleric who gave the interim council credibility, it was him. Najaf was also his home town and where he had trained as a cleric. For him the attack on the city was the last straw. At a press conference in Baghdad he argued that millions of moderates, who had welcomed the overthrow of Saddam Hussein the previous year, now regarded Washington as an enemy. 'The Americans have turned the holy city into a ghost town,' the dejected cleric said. 'They are now seen as full of hatred against Najaf and the Shia as Saddam Hussein was. Nothing will change this.' He said he did not understand why the United States had taken this action against Najaf, simply because of someone like Moqtada al Sadr. 'I don't know why America craves crisis, the long white-bearded elderly cleric said in exasperation. 'A peaceful solution to the confrontation with Moqtada could have been reached. We were hoping that Prime Minister Iyad Allawi would lead the way, but he sided with oppression.' Prime Minister Iyad Allawi had effectively given the order for the US and Iraqi army attack on Najaf.

Mohammed Bahr al Uloum had not always criticized US policy. He had, in fact, long been a harsh critic of Moqtada al Sadr, and attacked the young cleric for putting his own ambitions above the sanctity of Najaf. Bahr al Uloum's political credentials and his position as a respected senior cleric gave weight to his analysis of the attack. 'The [Iraqi interim] government has lost the support of the Middle Euphrates region and the south,' he said, 'even if it manages to calm down these areas temporarily using brute force. There is no wisdom to what the Americans and Allawi are doing. The consequences are unthinkable.'

These words came back to me when I was watching the news on an Arabic channel on the eve of Iraq's first ever general election in December 2005. The former interim Prime Minister and the candidate particularly favoured and promoted by the British government, Iyad Allawi, was speaking. It was Allawi's first visit to Najaf since the attack on the city one and a half years earlier. He was attempting to enhance his position among the Shia community and so his first port of call was, naturally enough, the Imam Ali shrine. Allawi, accompanied by a large entourage of officials and security men, went inside to pray.

News of his presence spread quickly around the compound of Imam Ali's tomb and in the nearby streets. By the time he had finished his prayers a crowd had gathered, and Allawi's security men tried to usher him out of the shrine as quickly as possible – there was certainly no time to shake hands and court voters. The hostile crowd surged forward, as young men grabbed at Allawi's clothes and a few even attempted to hit him. Then, just as they had done to the fallen statue of Saddam Hussein in Firdoos Square on the day that US forces took Baghdad, the young men took off their shoes and began hurling them at the interim prime minister. Footwear rained down and the crowd began to scream at the politician in their midst, this time not in jubilation but in rage. Allawi's entourage became more desperate as the mood grew more violent. This attack had not been planned; it was not an attempt by Moqtada al Sadr's henchmen to trap Allawi. The rage was too visceral, the desire to hurt Allawi too primal, the feelings of humiliation in the crowd too palpable. Allawi's bodyguards started firing into the air, to disperse the crowd, and along with Najaf's local police force managed to get Allawi out of the shrine. Jumping into bullet-proof cars they sped out of the city and headed away on the road back to Baghdad. When he had safely arrived back in the capital Allawi claimed that the attack at the shrine had been an assassination attempt. 'They were planning to kill the whole delegation,' before adding, 'or at least me.'

These were ordinary, unarmed citizens, visibly distressed by the destruction that had been inflicted on a sacred place. Without knowledge of the significance of Najaf, the event seems tragic, if unremarkable, in what has been a long-drawn-out war of great devastation. With the knowledge of Iraq's history, this scene is further proof of quite how significant Iraq is to Muslim identity.

Somalia is 99.95 per cent Muslim with a very small Christian community. Most Somali Muslims are Sunnis. In the nineteenth century Somalis were ethnically categorized as a 'Hamitic' people. It is really an invented category based on a racist aesthetic.

'Hamitic' literally means people who are believed to be descended from Ham, one of the Prophet Noah's four sons, who were, at one time, thought to have fathered the peoples of Africa. In truth the category was created by the European colonial authorities to distinguish what they believed were people who looked Semitic, whose features were more aquiline and gentle and who, to European sensibilities, looked more 'beautiful' than the negro and 'Bantu' peoples of Africa. The epithet was also intended to suggest that such people were superior to and more advanced than 'Bantu' Africans in that north-eastern part of the continent. 'Hamitic' people were pastoralist, camel- and goat-owning nomads, who travelled and thus came into contact and intermingled with Semitic civilizations to the north in the Arabian Peninsula and Egypt.

The truth is that Arab penetration of the north-eastern coastal areas of Africa, along present-day Somalia, Ethiopia, Eritrea and Sudan, goes back to at least the seventh century and many academics believe even earlier. Slavery had been a well-established practice among the tribes of the Arabian Peninsula even when Mohammed had been a young boy in Mecca towards the end of the sixth century, and it was the trade routes down to present-day Yemen and to Abyssinia (present-day Ethiopia) that provided the slaves for the clans and families in Arabian society. Abyssinia itself was an enormously powerful Christian kingdom which controlled present-day Yemen in alliance with the Byzantine Empire. In the year of the Prophet Mohammed's birth (estimated to be 570), the Abyssinian Emperor Abraha made an attempt to attack and sack the city of Mecca. His defeat is recorded in several verses of the Quran. The year was known as the Year of the Elephant, because Emperor Abraha's Abyssinian forces had been mounted on elephants when they were defeated.

Around 615, after the Prophet Mohammed had begun to receive the divine revelation of the Quran, and started to spread the monotheistic message of Islam in pagan pre-Islamic Mecca, many of Mohammed's then small group of converts had to flee. Mohammed's uncle and guardian, Abu Talib, was the head of the Banu Hashim clan, an important part of the Quraysh tribe who governed and controlled Mecca. As a result Mohammed had a level of protection from other members of the Quraysh who viewed him and his new monotheistic religion as a dangerous political and economic threat, as it undermined their control of the lucrative pilgrimages to Mecca's pagan shrines, most notably the Kaaba. Abu Talib's protection meant nobody could kill

Mohammed and avoid a legitimate demand for vengeance from the Banu Hashim.

However, this was not the case for many converts, who could be and were attacked. The weakest among all the converts were slaves, and the most prominent among them was an Abyssinian slave, Bilal. His master, determined to make Bilal renounce Islam, dragged him behind his horse through the desert, all the while ordering him to denounce Islam and the Prophet Mohammed. But Bilal kept shouting back at the top of his voice in Arabic: '*Ahad! Ahad!*', One, One. It was the only word Bilal was able to force out in his agony but it testified to his belief in the one, single deity of Allah.

Soon, however, the pressure on Abu Talib from the Meccan authorities to renounce and effectively give up Mohammed became too intense to bear. Economic sanctions were imposed on Mohammed and his followers; intermarriage was forbidden and trading with Muslims was banned. Abu Talib pleaded with his nephew: 'Spare me or spare yourself.' But Mohammed, of course, refused. Life became so intolerable for the early Muslims of Mecca that they had to leave. The Prophet had heard that the Christian king of Abyssinia, Ashamah, was a fair ruler so he allowed some of his followers to seek asylum there.

Fleeing from Mecca to Abyssinia, those Muslims would have had to cross, or at least travel close to, present-day Somaliland. There are many accounts of how the lands between present-day Ethiopia and Somalia and its peoples were a part of the story of the foundation of Islam at the time of the Prophet, even if the formal conversion of the Somali coastal regions and the explicit establishment of Islamic and Arabic cultures were due to Arab and also Persian settlement of these areas much later, in the ninth and tenth centuries. It was trade that brought the settlers, for slaves and for goods such as frankincense, gum arabic and myrrh that grow naturally and abundantly in Somaliland. Whenever I am home in Hargeisa I buy freshly harvested gum arabic in the stall in the market five minutes' walk from my parents' house and I have also bought it in Dire Dawa, Harar and the other main market towns across the border in eastern Ethiopia. Even now gum arabic is still an important export of Somaliland to the predominantly Muslim towns of eastern Ethiopia, only six hours' drive across the border.

The Somali coastal areas were important staging posts for Arab traders and explorers who would travel further south along the coast towards Zanzibar and the hinterland of the Swahili coast. Two ports of present-day Somaliland developed as a result of

the Arab settlements: Zeila and Berbera, the latter of
which is today the primary seaport for commercial
goods arriving in the country. In his *A Modern
History of the Somalia Nation*, I. M. Lewis says that
Zeila is mentioned in the writings of Arab geogra-
phers at the end of the ninth century as it is in the
records of al Ya'qubi. Trade in these ports extended
to include produce from the Abyssinian hinterland:
hides and skins, ivory, cloth, dates and pottery. As a
result, significant numbers of Arabs and to a lesser
extent Persians and Indians began to settle there, and
also in Mogadishu, further south along the coast.
The Arab settlers brought two things that would
leave a profound mark on Somali culture and identity: Islam and the Arabic language.

Most of the main clans that have been at the heart
of Somali social and political life are either descended
from or claim to be connected to lineages founded
by Arab settlers. All Somalis are taught from childhood to be able to recite their ancestral lineage back
to the founder of their clan. The custom, known as
'*Abtirsiimo*', which literally means the 'counting of
forebears', begins with your own name, followed by
that of your father, your grandfather, then his father
and so on. I can count back seventeen generations.
My own clan, the Isaq, are descended from Sheikh
Isaq, who arrived in Somalia from Arabia sometime

in the twelfth century and recounting the list
is almost as automatic as reciting the alphabet: beginning with Rageh, Abdullahi, Omaar, Awaleh,
Guleid, it ends with Sheikh Isaq Banu Ahmed Banu
Hashim. The last part of Sheikh Isaq's name identi-
fies him as a member of the same clan as the Prophet
Mohammed, the Banu Hashim.

Somali is a rich, mercurial hybrid language. Until
the latter half of the twentieth century it was a
completely oral language and it reflected the different peoples and cultures that have shaped Somalia.
It is littered with Arabic words as well as Hindi,
Persian, Amharric and Oromo from neighbouring
Ethiopia. A system for writing the Somali language
was formally introduced only in 1972, when the Siad
Barre regime set in motion a mass literacy campaign
as part of its programme to introduce 'Scientific
Socialism', a notion he had borrowed from his friend
Nicolae Ceauşescu, the Romanian dictator. Until
then, all Somali history, poetry, epic folk narratives
and tales, children's stories and family genealogy
were recorded orally. With the introduction of Islam
came the Arabic language, and nowadays Arabic is
still widely spoken in many places in Somalia and is
really an unofficial second language. Many people
then started using the Arabic script as a way of

writing down their language, in the way that it was used in Persia and Pakistan to write Farsi and Urdu. But the Arabic script was unsuitable for writing Somali because its vowel system was inadequate for many of the non-Arabic words in the language. And so a number of Somali elders, linguists and surprisingly open-minded teachers put the language into western Roman script, which proved to be perfect to transcribe the Somali language. This was more a triumph of inspired practicality than an indication that Somali culture and language were coming increasingly under the influence of Western intellectual systems.

The Quran is the immutable word of Allah, and cannot be changed, revised or altered in any way. There are no versions of the Quran, as there are of the Bible. However there are different customs and traditions attached to Islamic schools of thought, interpretation and custom. These orders are known as '*Tariqa*', which is the Arabic word for path, way or road. The principal Arab settlements in Somalia were taking place from the beginning of the tenth century, when Baghdad was not only the centre of the Islamic empire and Caliphate, but also one of the principal intellectual centres of the world and a commercial and cultural crossroads. It was in

Baghdad and Basra that the main schools of Sufism began to emerge. Although it can be traced back several centuries, it was in the tenth century that the most influential and celebrated schools and traditions of Sufism were developed in Baghdad and Basra. These schools and their adherents dispersed throughout the Islamic world at that time, and it was through them that Islam as a religion was firmly implanted in much of the Horn of Africa. Although the Arab settlers and traders were Muslims themselves, which meant that indigenous people along the Somali coast came into contact with Muslims, it was the Sufis who brought and spread the religion itself. Thanks to them, by the thirteenth and fourteenth centuries, present-day Somalia had been converted and Islam had been firmly established.

Three of these Sunni Sufi traditions are dominant in Somalia today. The oldest is the Qadiriyah, the oldest such order in Islam, which was founded by Sheikh Abd al Qadir Jilani. My mother's surname is Abd al Qadir and her family can trace a connection back to the first adherents of the Qadiriyah tradition, which originated in Baghdad.

In 1997 I moved to Amman, Jordan for the BBC. From the outset I was drawn to events in Iraq. It had been nearly seven years since Saddam Hussein's disastrous invasion of Kuwait and the subsequent war to force Iraq to withdraw its troops from the Gulf emirate. The consequences of that conflict and seven years of punitive economic sanctions had destroyed much of the country's social and economic fabric but had done nothing to diminish Saddam Hussein's control of its people and their lives. I received my first visa for Iraq in September 1997. Before I set off on the journey by road into Saddam Hussein's Iraq, I telephoned my mother in Hargeisa. It was her first time back in Somaliland after the civil war, which had ended only a few months before the first Gulf War came to an end. The experience had left her in a state of shock. I remember her saying during that telephone conversation that she envied me. 'I wish I could come with you,' she said. 'I wish I could go to Baghdad in your suitcase.' I told her she was probably the only mother of a BBC correspondent who wanted to accompany her child to Iraq, not because she wanted to protect me, but because she wanted to see the country and its capital herself.

In 1995, my mother and I had gone on holiday to Jordan to visit a cousin of my mother who worked for the United Nations. During our stay my mother asked me to take her across the Allenby Bridge to the West Bank so that she could go to Jerusalem and

pray at the Al Aqsa mosque. For two days, during
the Muslim holy day of Friday and the Sabbath, my
mother prayed for six hours each day. She told me
then that she desperately wanted to go to Baghdad
to complete the trilogy of pilgrimages to what she
regarded as the most important sites in the Islamic
tradition: Mecca, Jerusalem and, as a Qadariyah
Sunni, the mosque of Sheikh Abd al Qadir Jilani in
Baghdad. 'Promise me that you will try to visit it
during your trip,' she urged me again two years later,
'and try to bring some pictures. Oh how I'd love to
see it!'

She ended the conversation with a familiar lecture
and I listened with a mixture of fond exasperation
and amusement: 'One more thing, and just listen to
me this time! Listen, we will all have to recount our
lives before God when we leave this earth, Rageh.'
I tried, as always, to head off the conversation, saying
I knew what she was going to say and that I took
her point but . . . 'Listen to me,' she said forcefully,
'your career, journalism awards, fancy titles, all that
will mean nothing on Judgement Day. What matters
is have you lived life as a true and honest Muslim?'
Then her tone changed from one of mild scolding
to seriousness. I stopped trying to interrupt when
she said, 'You are very fortunate. You have the
opportunity to go to a place which many Muslims

would give much to be able to see. You have the chance to say prayers for your family and all your forebears, and to give thanks and ask for blessings for all of them in a place that is very, very important. Go to the Abd al Qadir Jilani mosque, and pray there, because you may never get that chance again. None of your family has had that chance.'

On the eastern Al Rusafah bank of the Tigris river in Baghdad lies one of the oldest quarters of the city, a district known as Bab Al Sheikh, the Gate of the Sheikh. A maze of rough-tracked back alleys, just about wide enough for a small car to nudge its way past the gangs of mischievous young boys who play makeshift football between the houses and stand to the side to watch as you pass by. Stout metal gates lead into the yards of the low, squat houses where women scrub the family laundry in large metal troughs. Bab Al Sheikh is a poor district and most of the people work on the neighbourhood market stalls and in the local bakeries and hardware shops. Bab Al Sheikh owes its existence to the shrine of Sheikh Abd al Qadir Jilani, which lies at the very heart of the neighbourhood. As in the other holy sites of Najaf and Karbala, the crowded streets and alleys seem to have sprung from the mosque like the branches of a tree.

The compound of Abd al Qadir Jilani comprises a mosque, a shrine to the sheikh himself and a *madrassa*. On my first trip to Iraq in 1997 I walked down one of Bab Al Sheikh's roughly paved alleys that runs alongside the walls of the shrine and eventually leads to one of two main gates. The crowds at the entrance, many of whom were kissing the gates as they entered and left, made it hard for me to squeeze inside the courtyard but once I had disentangled myself I emerged into a wide, open space where people who had finished their prayers were sitting on the cobbled ground talking quietly as their young children ran in circles around them. Close to the mosque the courtyard rose slightly and a short flight of steps led me to the *mirhab*, the small, decorated alcove where Muslim clerics lead the faithful in prayers. This outside *mirhab* was used for summertime prayers, in order to escape the intolerable swelter of the Iraqi summer.

To the side of one of the two minarets was a tall, thin clock tower; an addition which dates from the end of the nineteenth century. Standing among the families milling around and the children playing between prayer times, the clock tower gave the courtyard the atmosphere of a public square or a university campus.

In the central prayer hall, lined with a rich oxbloodred carpet inlaid with flowers picked out in thin white thread, lay the tomb of Sheikh Abd al Qadir Jilani, its wooden entrance decorated with a fine Ottoman lattice frame. The Sheikh's wooden sarcophagus was housed in a stone and marble tomb inscribed with an Arabic dedication.

I first visited this shrine not as a journalist, or to interview a cleric, even if it was a journalistic assignment that had brought me to the country. I went to Abd al Qadir Jilani's shrine because I had been told by my family that we were connected to this place. I went there never expecting to feel that connection. I went, I suppose, because of my own curiosity and to please my mother. Yet as I stood in the courtyard, I did feel that cultural thread which linked my family to something much larger and which went beyond the borders of a small, unrecognized, impoverished republic in the Horn of Africa.

Iraq connects us all. It connects us to the story of the Prophet Mohammed's descendants. It connects us to the story of how Islam broke out of Arabia and became a global religion. It connects us to the story of how Islam was established from a small corner of north-eastern Africa to Asia. Dig deep enough into the family history of most Muslims, whether they are Sunni or Shia, and I am confident that you will find stories like that of my mother's family. The assault on Iraq has given extremist groups linked to Al Qaeda a chance to explore the anger of ordinary Muslims at what they see as an attack on the cultural and historical things they hold most dear.

For many Muslims the Iraq war represents a direct assault on their identity, a sentiment that seems inevitable when you take into account the connection between Iraq and Islam's beginnings. And if, in retrospect, it appears foolhardy for the British government not to have taken a greater interest in the history of the region and its significance for Muslims, then it seems even more extraordinary than Britain's own history of its dealings in Iraq seems to have had no bearing on the British government's policies in recent years.

At the beginning of the twentieth century Iraq, then called Mesopotamia, was part of the Ottoman Empire. In 1914, when Britain discovered that Turkey was joining the First World War on the side of Germany, it set out to eradicate Turkish control of the region. The British invaded from the south, capturing Basra, and decided to carry on north to Baghdad. But the campaign was long, hard and costly in terms of lives and resources. Three years later, General Angus Maude, the commander of British forces in Mesopotamia, captured Baghdad.

The city fell in March 1917. As soon as they took control, the British authorities issued a declaration, written in Arabic and circulated throughout the city, which read: 'To the people of Baghdad. Our armies do not come in your cities and lands as conquerors, but as liberators, so that we may free you from generations of tyranny.' General Maude said that Britain intended to give Iraq control of its own affairs. It took more than a year for Britain to gain control of the northern regions of the country, as far as Mosul.

Arab nationalists in Iraq who had demanded independence had supported the Allied invasion believing that getting rid of the Ottoman regime would bring this about swiftly. The Allies had no such intention. After the end of the First World War, at the Paris Peace Conference in 1919, Iraq was formally made a mandate entrusted to Britain under the League of Nations Covenant. The same thing happened to another Middle Eastern territory, Palestine. This new Iraq was to be run by a British High Commissioner, Sir Percy Cox. Then things started to go wrong. Sunni tribal groups, Shia religious authorities in Najaf and Karbala agitated against British rule, and the rebellious central and southern parts of Iraq descended into chaos and began to slip from British control. But the most acute problem facing the British was the growing anger of the nationalists, who felt betrayed that the British had not left but had taken possession of Iraq as a mandate territory. An insurgency broke out. One secret underground insurgency group based in Najaf and calling itself 'The Gathering of the Islamic Awakening' carried out the assassination of a British officer. There was a call for an uprising against the British, mainly led by the Shia clergy in Najaf.

Upon the death of a leading Shia cleric in early May 1920, Sunni and Shia set aside their differences and urged people to rise up. Najaf was surrounded. Violent demonstrations followed when the British tried to arrest some Shia clerics. The rebellion spread, reaching as far north as Mosul. The British forces asked for reinforcements from India and Persia. The most ferocious resistance was in the central Euphrates plains, and so as part of the military campaign to break the back of the insurgency, the British bombarded a city called Fallujah.

The 1920 revolt proved extremely costly in money, men, materials and political standing for Britain, and inevitably domestic criticism of the campaign began to be voiced in Whitehall and the country at large. Britain then decided to replace the military government running Iraq with something it called a provisional government, to prepare the country for eventual self-government. The pro-visional government would have British advisers but was still answerable to Sir Percy Cox. The Prime Minister, Lloyd George, was challenged to pull British troops out of Iraq, but replied that if they did 'withdraw from Iraq there would be chaos and civil war'.

We are all trapped within Iraq's history. There is something of all of us in its story.

5. Hidden Lives

I remember the date because it was my birthday. My aunt Sophia called on the morning of 19 July 2005 but, as it turned out, it wasn't to wish me a happy birthday. I remember I was in the middle of packing for a trip to Ethiopia to visit my relatives who settled there after fleeing northern Somalia many years earlier. Sophia had just heard some news and needed me to pass it on to the family I was going to see in a few days' time. 'Asha's nephew has been attacked by a gang. It happened about ten days ago I think. He was rushed to hospital. His throat was cut and the family believe it was because he was a Muslim. No other reason. I just spoke to Asha but she didn't want to talk for long. The young boy is very seriously ill.'

Although my aunt was speaking quickly and was obviously in a panic she spelled out the details of what had happened deliberately and precisely. I found it impossible to believe. A relative of ours: an intelligent, quiet, reserved individual who had happily settled in Britain had had his throat slit in London because he was a Muslim? My aunt had used a specific Somali word, '*goracaay*', pronounced 'gow-ra'ay'. It is a term used by butchers in reference to animals. Halal butchers kill animals without the use of machines or electric shock but by a method that is centuries old: slitting the animal's throat as they offer up a prayer of thanks to God. '*Goracaay*' is a word most often heard around the time of Eid at the end of the fasting month of Ramadan when a sheep is sacrificed by a halal butcher. The only time I had heard the term used in relation to human beings was in conversations about politics at home, when a ruthless dictatorship had presided over the mass slaughter of civilians. But my aunt was using it now, about a relative, in London.

'What do you mean he had his throat slit?' I asked. She repeated the story. My aunt had less of a problem in accepting that this could happen in Britain in 2005 than I did. I'd spent the past thirteen years witnessing almost exactly the same thing in countless places around the world and putting such images on television, but I found it difficult to accept that it could occur here. 'Well, it happened soon after the bombings in London. You've seen all the attacks on Muslims around the country, the stoning and attempted fire bombings of mosques. Of course it could be because he was Muslim.' She paused for a moment, then said firmly, 'It had to be because he was a Muslim!'

Asha's family are cousins of my father. In Somali culture first cousins are akin to brothers and sisters, and as a result, Asha and her husband, Osman, are my aunt and uncle. At the end of the 1980s, as the Somali civil war raged and the regime of Siad Barre bombarded Hargeisa they, like tens of thousands of others, fled with their four children on foot across the Ogaden desert towards Ethiopia. Asha and her youngest son became so exhausted and weak that the rest of the family had to push them in a wheelbarrow across the wild savannah plains for hundreds of miles towards the Ethiopian frontier. They were granted asylum in Britain and settled in north London. They have been very close to my immediate family ever since.

In 2004 a nephew of Asha, Mohammed Ahmed

Ismail, was staying with them temporarily while he waited for accommodation to be provided by his local housing office. He was eventually given a bedsit in Hackney which became his home, but he had by then become very close to Asha, her husband and two children (the other two had grown up and left home), and would often visit for a few days. On 7 July 2005, when the four suicide bombers exploded their bombs in London, Mohammed was staying at Asha's house. Three days later he headed back to his flat in Hackney.

It was about eight o'clock on a warm July evening and the sun had not yet set. As he approached his block of flats he was accosted by a group of young men. There had been no intimation of the violence before it happened. In fact, my cousin hadn't felt threatened at all. Before he had time to think the men had surrounded him. They pulled out knives from beneath their jackets and descended upon him, slashing at his flesh, battering him to the ground. They slammed his head on the pavement and cut the skin of his shoulders, thighs, ears, forearms and hands. One stab severed a muscle in his calf. How many of them were there? Five, six? He does not know because the attack was so sudden. He lost consciousness when they cut his throat. Then they were interrupted. A white woman was driving past.

When she saw what was happening she stopped the car and began to scream as loudly as she could. She shouted at the attackers to stop, letting them know that she could see what was happening. The men fled, and then the woman saw the blood. Streams of red poured from Mohammed's body as he lay unconscious on the pavement. She screamed for help. A crowd gathered and an ambulance was called. Mohammed was taken to the intensive care unit of the Royal London Hospital in Aldgate. He fell into a coma as surgeons tried to stabilize his condition and operate on his wounds.

Mohammed would be in hospital for two months. The severed muscle in his calf could not be repaired and he is still on crutches. It is uncertain whether he will ever be able to walk unaided. He continues to ask himself questions about the attack. Were they waiting for a Muslim or him in particular? Had they been drinking? Did they mistake him for someone else? He does not know and the uncertainty means he is very anxious whenever he is walking on the street near his home. At the time of writing there has been no conclusion to the police investigation.

About two weeks after the attack on Mohammed, two cousins of my aunt Asha, sisters called Habiba and Asha too, went to visit Mohammed at the Royal London Hospital. The sisters are in their mid-fifties and dress traditionally in long Islamic gowns and headscarves. They set off early as they had to travel across London from Hounslow in the west to the Royal London Hospital in the east. They took the underground, and then caught a bus from the train station that would take them close to the hospital. It was the end of July, the attempted bombings of the 21st had just happened. The two sisters sat next to each other on the bus, absorbed in their own conversation, not noticing the other passengers on the lower deck. The bus arrived at their stop near the hospital and they got off. However, when they reached the wing where Mohammed was staying, the staff nurse turned them back saying Mohammed's visiting hours were severely restricted because he had just come out of intensive care and needed as much rest as possible. Disappointed and annoyed with themselves that they had not checked with the hospital before setting out, Asha and Habiba left and crossed the road to the bus stop on the other side.

They had been standing there waiting for about ten minutes when they saw the first vehicle speeding towards them, as though it intended to run them down. As it got closer they realized it was a police car. Suddenly there was another one. Two large police vans skidded in front of them, positioning themselves so as to block the road. They were full of flak-jacketed police officers, some of whom were armed. The officers burst out of the vans and ran towards the two women. In one moment they had grabbed Asha and Habiba and pulled their arms behind their backs. The two women were terrified, trying to calm the police officers down but also desperate to know why they were being restrained. Everything happened very quickly and at least two policemen patted them down beneath their dresses and searched their handbags. As the two women stood shaking on the street an officer took down their names and addresses, and when Asha and Habiba asked why this was happening a policeman replied that they were not able to disclose any information but that a police liaison officer would be in touch. Finally the officers got back in their vans and drove away. A bus arrived and Asha and Habiba climbed on board, watched nervously by people on the street.

Asha and Habiba have lived in the UK for eleven years. Before coming to Britain they lived and were educated for many years in Zimbabwe where their family owned a business. Their husbands' businesses had brought them to Britain and they had settled here not as refugees but as wives of middle-class businessmen. Their appearance, as middle-aged, conservative African Muslim women, may have made people think that they were meek and possibly illiterate, at the mercy of a patriarchal culture, but in fact they are educated, self-possessed women. They had taken down the names of the officers who had accosted them and when they got home they telephoned the authorities to demand an explanation. The story which emerged is incredible.

On the bus from the station to the hospital fellow passengers and an undercover transport policeman had noticed Asha and Habiba sitting next to each other on the lower deck. There was something about the two women that worried the passengers and someone called the police saying they thought they could be terrorists. Asha and Habiba asked the police what had led people to that conclusion. The officers told them that witnesses on the bus had reported that one of them seemed to be carrying something bulky under her dress. The officer added that many of the people on the bus, including the undercover transport policeman, could not understand why they would be wearing 'such clothes', meaning their Muslim headscarves and long dark gowns, on a summer day in July. Surely even they would wear 'lighter material' on a hot day? The police now accepted that the people on the bus had made a mistake; and that the reason why Asha looked as though she was carrying a suspect backpack and

Habiba did not, was because Asha was overweight and had a thick waist and big hips, whereas her sister Habiba was thinner. That's what the problem was: being fat and a Muslim.

Since then Habiba and Asha have often remarked how lucky they were that things had not gone more wrong, that the Metropolitan Police's shoot-to-kill policy had not been enacted on that day too.

This is the first time the stories of Mohammed, Asha and Habiba have appeared in print. No reporter has come to their house to hear their stories. No one from *Woman's Hour* has interviewed them. Their stories are apparently not important.

When people in public life, be they politicians, political journalists or film-makers, use language which portrays a minority as behaving in a way which is beneath the accepted standards of the majority, when they use language which conveys that minority as believing in a religion which is *inherently* backward, they act as the handmaidens of violent racist philosophy. They give legitimacy to those who would like to 'drive out' those whose identity and beliefs they despise. Mohammed Ahmed Ismail and his family are among hundreds of victims of the same words and impulses, whether uttered by right-wing British groups, novelists, journalists or European MEPs. The language of people in positions of influence cannot be separated from the social and political climate of everyday life. Of course, commentators who are exercising their legitimate right to free speech when they condemn Islam or hold Muslims up to ridicule are not wielding knives against a young Somali man or even calling the police when they see an overweight, middle-aged Muslim woman on a bus and jump to the conclusion that she is a terrorist, but they must realize that their actions at a time when a minority is at its most vulnerable may feed the bigotry of people less rational or educated than themselves.

Ealing Town Hall is housed in a large brown functional-looking building off the High Street of the west London borough. A short walk away, on the other side of the council car park, is a two-storey row of offices which house Ealing Racial Equality Council. The office feels anonymous. People sit quietly at banks of computers surrounded by high filing cabinets, tapping away earnestly at their keyboards, lending the room the solemn atmosphere of a university library. A woman in a neat dark suit, dreadlocks piled high on her head and tightly bound in a headscarf, comes out to meet me at reception. She gives me a small smile. 'I know you,' she says. 'It's a long way from Ealing to Iraq!' she giggles warmly. 'You must be here to see Asha. Have a seat. I'll give her a tinkle and let her know you're here.' A few minutes later, Asha Ali Yassin walks down the corridor. She is tall with a very light complexion typical of many Somalis as a result of centuries of intermarriage with Arabs. Her complexion would be described as 'red' in Somali – the colour associated with the people who live in the Arabian Peninsula. Somalis with light complexions hate being described as 'blond' or Caucasian-looking.

Asha is a senior officer of the council's anti-racial harassment project. She has lived in Britain for nearly twenty-five years, and there is no trace of Somali accent in her English. She was born and grew up in Kenya, where there is a large Somali population, and fell in love and married a man from the north of Somalia. She trained as a teacher in Kenya and has always led an active professional life, as many Somali women from different generations have. She came to Britain when her husband was posted to work in the Somali embassy. Her children were born and raised in Britain, as both British and Somali. By the mid-1980s, when the Siad Barre dictatorship's human rights abuses were at their height, and the war against the main tribes in the rebellious north of the country had begun, Asha's husband, disgusted by and disillusioned with his government like millions of other Somalis, resigned his position at the embassy in protest, and applied for asylum in Britain, which was granted. The late 1980s were the peak years for the arrival of Somali refugees in Britain, especially from the north, the region which Britain ruled as a protectorate. The intricate and closely bound clan system meant that in the Somali community most people were either related to or knew someone who was claiming asylum.

Asha possessed a rare combination of skills and experience which made her very useful to both the incoming refugee population and the British authorities: she was completely bilingual, she was a trained professional who had by then spent around seven years in Britain and was at ease in the country, her children had grown up here, and also, as a woman, she was able to communicate with and counsel other Somali women who for cultural and religious reasons would be very uncomfortable talking to men about their traumatic experiences during the conflict. She decided to go to work for what was then the British Refugee Council, and is now the Refugee Council. By the early 1990s, after the peak years of immigration, as Somalis began to settle, the needs and priorities of the refugee community naturally shifted. Asha left the Refugee Council and went on to work at a Citizens Advice Bureau in

Hanwell, west London, where she gave advice to Somalis on matters such as education, housing, discrimination and employment and training regulations. In 1996 she began working with Hounslow council's monitoring group, which deals exclusively with victims of racial harassment. In 1999 she moved to her current job with Ealing council's racial harassment unit.

I could see all the reasons why she would want to work on asylum and immigration, but wondered why she had focused on racial harassment. 'Well . . . one obviously leads to the other. That's true with almost all immigrant communities. However, there was a big difference in the experience of Somalis. In the years after the main waves of immigration, as Somali communities settled all over Britain, as children began to be born and raised here, we faced all the disadvantages that other communities did, and we did so with no leadership. We were too fragmented, too disorganized to have a voice or even a place where we could talk about our common problems. It made me want to do something.' The attacks of 7th July exacerbated the situation. 'There is now both racial and religious hate,' she says. 'Somalis are very distinct, you can spot them a mile off; not only because of what they look like physically, but also because of their clearly Muslim appearance – women generally dress conservatively in scarves and headdresses, and many men have beards.'

Young Somalis face the greatest problems of all. 'Young Somali boys came and are still coming to Britain typically at the age of nine, ten or eleven. Obviously they don't speak English, and most have never been to the West and have little idea about what it's like. Within a matter of months, just as their families begin their new lives in an entirely different world, they as children find themselves with another new world of their own in the form of school.' As Asha said this I thought of my own family and those close friends who have settled in Britain as refugees. The one thing that parents always say has been the most positive and rewarding aspect of their new lives in Britain is the opportunity of giving their children a western education, and all that entails in terms of genuine social progress.

But Asha points out that while that is true in the longer run for most families, the most significant causes of alienation, economic failure and eventual petty crime among those young Somalis who are unable to adapt to immigrant life and integrate into British society often have their roots in the early stages of their life at school. Failure at school – both socially and, often as a consequence, academically –

not only alienates children from their peers but also from their parents, their one piece of solid ground in an unfamiliar world. 'You have to try to imagine what it must be like from the point of view of this newly arrived nine- or ten-year-old Somali boy at his local school. He can barely speak the language, he doesn't understand other children and what the teachers are saying to him, he's probably scared and he sticks out like a sore thumb as there are probably very few other children like him in the school. He's Muslim, yet he's completely different from the Asian kids, he's black but he's very different from the Afro-Caribbean kids too, and he can't communicate with either group anyway. In this context it's inevitable that he'll be picked on; after all, he's the odd one, the strange one, who can't say anything.'

Her words made me remember my own childhood, things I had not thought about for years. My experience was very different as I had not come to Britain as a refugee and was sent to a private school. However, if you are a child who is different from everyone else in the class *and* you are unable to express yourself, it does not take long before you begin to hate yourself and the reasons why you find yourself in this position. All children face powerful pressures to fit in at school. Somali refugee children will often find these pressures unbearable and will either completely adopt the identity of the other children and rid themselves as much and as demonstrably as they can of the culture and identity which have made them so alien, or they will despise and reject the dominant group. 'When a young Somali boy is bullied at school he may react in the way he has seen people act in a war zone. He may have seen people killed, he may have seen people in refugee camps beating and shoving his mother or sisters in the queues lining up to receive their rations and he reacts as others did there: they fight, they argue, they try to impose their will in order to survive, but most of all, they fight to ensure they won't be humiliated again.'

Children who behave like this in class are, of course, reported or their parents are called to the school. Somali parents are horrified that their child is squandering his chances and their first reaction is to blame him. 'You know what Somali parents would say in the context,' Asha says. 'They have just come to Britain, here is this amazing, life-changing opportunity put in front of their child, why are they throwing it away? They should get on, keep quiet, not mess things up. Newly arrived immigrant parents are often very deferential towards educational and health authorities, because to them, Western education and Western medicine are . . . well, they are just the centre of their dreams. Their instinct is not to listen to the stories of the child. By the time young men in this position reach sixteen, all their thoughts are on getting the hell out of this environment and system, and as soon as they reach sixteen, they leave school never to come back.'

Asha then remembered the story of a young Somali man she had known. 'You know I could see from very early on that this boy was going to get into serious trouble and serious problems,' she said. 'He left school and I used to see him hanging around Ealing High Street now and again. I could just see that sooner or later something would happen, he was hanging around with other young men . . . you get the idea. Eventually, he was arrested and he was given a custodial sentence. The first I knew about it was when he started writing to me from prison. It was terrible, because there was nothing I could do about it. I just saw the slow and inevitable collapse of this young guy. A few years later, I saw him again. He had written to tell me he was being released. He hit the booze as soon as he got out. The sad thing was that he still had the remnants of the traditional Somali respect for elders and he wrote and talked to me as if I was an older sister, someone with a position in society. He'd try not to be obvious about his drinking, as if he was still a teenager trying to hide the smell of alcohol on his breath from his father. He was also smoking hashish. He was sinking.

'One day he called me and said: "Asha could you give me some money, I need to get something to eat and I'm skint," but I knew full well he wanted it for booze or to buy some more hashish, so I said, "No, but I tell you what, I will take you out and we'll have lunch together." He agreed, a bit grudgingly, after he had tried again to make me give him the money. I took him to a local restaurant, a sort of Balti house. I knew he wanted money because he wasn't really that hungry, but I went ahead and began ordering something for both of us. I will never forget what he said that day, it just hit me in the stomach. "I don't eat chicken, Asha." He said it very emphatically. I didn't think much of it, presuming it was because he was allergic or something, so I said, "Oh, why not? You don't have to worry. It's halal chicken here." He fiddled with his cutlery and looked down at the table. "I don't eat chicken," he said, "because they called me chicken legs when I was at school. I didn't know what they meant at the time because I couldn't speak English, but I never forgot the words. Later on, when I learned what chicken legs were, I decided never to eat chicken again."' That was the last Asha saw of him.

Almost immediately, Asha recalled another story

from many years ago, before she began to work with cases of racial harassment. 'It was when I used to work as an interpreter for social services. I was called to interpret at St Bernard's, which is a mental health hospital in this area. There was a young disabled Somali girl who had been sectioned. She had a large family and a blazing row had broken out at home. The police had been called and when they arrived they found a crowd of people shouting at each other. The young girl was caught in the middle, and like everyone else she was screaming and shouting. She was on crutches, and was using her crutches to make her point and to keep people at a distance. The police just saw a deranged, crippled girl, aggressively waving her metal crutches; they could not understand a word she said. She was sectioned there and then and her family couldn't understand what was happening. There was absolutely nothing wrong with her mind.

'Luckily for her, with God's good grace, her psychiatrist was an Iraqi exile. She felt calmer and less alienated from him, and he had a natural empathy with her as a young Muslim woman in this situation, but she was in a real state and would shout and scream and refuse to follow instructions. I was called to interpret. The young girl leapt at me: "I'm not mad! I'm not ill! Please tell them there's nothing wrong with me. Please get me out of here!" She couldn't stop talking and was clearly in a great state. The Iraqi doctor pulled me aside once I translated the girl's detailed story of what had happened. "Listen!" he told me. "You have to tell her that she has to stop shouting, stop being so aggressive, otherwise she won't get out of here for a long time. I know she must be frightened, she must feel humiliated as a Muslim woman in this environment, but she can't wave her crutches around. She mustn't shout out at people or throw her medication on the floor. In this system, you have to show that there is nothing wrong with you." I translated very carefully, and the Iraqi doctor followed up her case. Thank God she was eventually discharged. I saw her four years later. She had married and had settled down and was planning on starting a family.'

Young Somali girls, Asha points out, face different yet graver dangers which are almost never reported or investigated. Somalis are a conservative Muslim community, and parents are very strict about girls going out in the evenings. This protectiveness stems not only from the natural concern of a parent for a vulnerable young daughter in a city, but is also part of Somali culture. However, Somali girls, like all girls, find ways of escaping these strictures: they sneak out of windows late at night, or they say they are going to stay the night at the house of other young girls, where the restrictions may not be as tight as in their own households.

'I liaise very closely with the police in Ealing, and they say that reports are increasing of young Somali girls who are getting attacked in unlicensed mini-cabs. These minicabs are obviously cheaper and at three or four in the morning it's the only way to get home from the club or disco or party they've been to. The police say that many of them report being molested, and nearly raped. But there is no way they can report this to their families. How can they explain *how* it happened, let alone *what* has happened. The police say the young girls who come to them, do so in order to inform the police about the minicab drivers so they can keep an eye on them in the hope that the same thing doesn't happen to other young girls. But when they're urged to bring a formal charge, they don't, because they feel they can't. It's an awful vicious circle which is happening every week. The worst thing is, of course, that it makes young Somali girls even *more* of a target, even more vulnerable. Word gets round some of these drivers: doing this to Somali girls runs less risk. They're pretty, they're always desperate to get home *and* they don't say anything.

'What could capture our situation more clearly

than what is happening to these young Somali girls? They are trapped by traditional customs from Somalia which haven't yet adapted to their new lives in Britain on the one hand, and yet they are exposed to the same dangers that all young women face in a modern, urban society. They have no voice. It will come, but it will be long and slow, and as far as I can see at the moment, we are going to have to do it entirely on our own.'

But there are signs of hope. In Ealing, where Asha works, young Somalis have opened a club, a combination of café, meeting place and centre for community activities. It's called Talow, which means advice and opinion, and it provides a valuable service. Young men who have done time at young offenders' institutions such as Feltham and have become very devout Muslims, could easily, without a place like Talow, turn their sense of marginalization into violence, as Yassin Hassan Omar did. Other, more secular, young men are trying to build up a network of small local businesses. Others believe that the only way they can begin to make their voices heard is to mobilize their numbers – not through demonstrations or protests, but by voting. Boroughs such as Ealing and many other districts in cities such as Sheffield, Cardiff and Manchester have very considerable Somali populations, only a tiny number of whom are registered voters. If even half the eligible Somali voters would vote in national and local elections, they could easily influence or determine the election of at least fifteen MPs. There are many young Somalis who realize the power and voice such political organization would very quickly bring.

Asha is working with the young men who share the backgrounds of Britain's suicide bombers: marginalized angry young men, many of whom have been in and out of prison. Men who are easily influenced, who are often either physically miles away from their family and past or are alienated from them and who are seeking something else to bind them to their community or give them a purpose. Men who are lost and whose rage is heightened by what seems to be further condemnation of them and the one thing that gives them an identity: Islam. I ask Asha what she thinks of the response to Muslims in the West and the elevation of people such as Ayaan Hersi Ali as a spokesperson for Somalis and Muslims in Europe. 'Why is she given a platform to speak about a group of people she despises? Answer me why? She is not the future for Somalis and Muslims in Europe, and she is not the future for Europeans who will have to live in a world with us. Love her. Promote her. Be enchanted by her. But she is not our future.'

6. Voices

In October 2005, in the run-up to the Muslim holy month of Ramadan, I went to Hounslow to visit an aunt who immigrated to Britain nine years ago as a refugee from the war in Somalia. I sat on the lower deck of the bus looking out as we passed the curry houses and vegetable stalls on Southall's High Street, home to a large number of Somalis and many British Asians, many of whom work at Heathrow airport, which is close by. It was a cold and dark afternoon, the kind of winter's day when it seems the sun has struggled to rise at all. Suddenly I was aware of eight teenage schoolgirls tumbling down from the top deck, shouting and laughing. Some were white girls, but several were young

Somalis, their heads neatly wrapped in dark head-scarves, their uniforms consisting of very tight drainpipe trousers and fake Chanel bags with shiny interlocking buckles slung over their shoulders, glimmering in the glare of the bus's strip lighting. Their loud and high-pitched chatter jumped from one another to their mobile phones that jangled out in the otherwise utterly silent bus. The Somali girls switched back and forth, in and out, from a thick London accent to Somali. One of them turned to her white friend and screeched: 'Those bacon crisps are disgusting! Just keep that minging smell away from me girl, I tell ya!' and then fell about laughing. They discussed each other's clothes and another girl in their class, then one of the Somali girls shouted, '*Bisinka!* Did you really say that?' In one breath she went from a Somali Muslim word, '*Bisinka*', which means 'By God's Mercy', or 'With God's help', and which Somalis use when something shocking happens, to English. None of her friends, black, white or Muslim, batted an eyelid.

My aunt is in her fifties and is a devout Muslim, praying five times a day without fail, and like the young girls on the bus, she was also wearing a Muslim headscarf. I told her the scene on the bus, thinking she would find it as enjoyable as I had, but she was unusually quiet and in fact didn't see what I was laughing about. 'They're so loud when they're coming home in the afternoon, those school children on the buses,' she said disapprovingly. I soon learned that she had had a bad day and an experience on the bus that was far from pleasant.

My aunt had gone on her weekly shop on the High Street with a Somali friend. On the way back they planned to look in on a friend who had recently been bereaved (bereavement means you are never left alone for a moment and can expect visitors day and night). The two women had been sitting on the long bank of seats by the door when a white man boarded the bus and sat next to my aunt. The problem was that my aunt had done her ablutions for her daily prayers that morning, a process that is laborious and time-consuming and she didn't want to have to do them twice. Once the ablutions are complete the rule, for men and women, is that you mustn't touch a member of the opposite sex who is not your relative until you have completed your prayers. My aunt got up to sit somewhere else because it was a tight squeeze on the seat and with their shopping bags too it was difficult to keep their distance.

'The man went crazy. He started shouting,' she said. '"You are so rude! How dare you? It should be *me* who moves away from *you* given how your type blows up buses. You are the intolerant ones!"

He was so hysterical and there was such a scene, that I couldn't explain that it was only because of my ablutions that we had moved away. That we didn't mean anything by it. It was nothing to do with him being white or non-Muslim.' My aunt was clearly very shaken by the experience but was not angry. She just wished she could have explained to the man why she had moved away from him. Now he would never know.

These two episodes, happening on the same day, in the same part of London, give us an insight into the future and the options that are available to all of us if we are prepared to make the right decisions. Islam is reputed to be the fastest growing religion in Western societies and Muslims are not going to disappear from our towns and cities. If our societies are to thrive, our knowledge of the people who live among us has to improve. Throughout my adult life and more particularly since September 11 I have seen Muslims represented only in broad brush strokes: in articles about fundamentalism; in speeches about the need for reform; in news broadcasts about secularism versus religion; on the clash of civilizations, of good versus evil. The voice of the individual has been lost and without it nothing is understood.

The young Somali girls on the bus were not alien

or frightening to their friends despite the fact that they wore headscarves, were a different colour, spoke a different language. In fact those young white schoolgirls are probably more connected to the lives of British Muslims than any politician or newspaper editor. On the other hand, my aunt's action was a consequence of her devout beliefs – which seem no odder to me than a Jewish man wearing a skullcap or perhaps a Catholic eating and drinking the body and blood of Christ – and yet her fellow passenger was appalled by her actions. Muslims are unfamiliar to and seen as alien by so many people in this country, their experiences as individuals whether working as a travel agent on a high street or living as a mother in a suburb, as a recently arrived refugee or as an educated woman in a youth centre, or as a businessman in Edgware Road are rarely heard. And yet, without allowing these voices in politics, on our streets, in our schools, in our newspapers and on our televisions we are all lost. It is only when the voice of the individual is lifted above the waves of condemnation that all of us can begin to see more clearly and perhaps start to realize that our worlds are not actually in conflict after all.

7. The Veil

A year later

Dewsbury lies by the River Calder in West Yorkshire, nestled among dark, rugged hills, nine miles from Leeds. In the nineteenth century its fortunes grew as it became a mill town for England's wool industry and it expanded to accommodate the rising number of mill workers. In the late 1950s, and up until the early 1970s, many poor families from South Asia and particularly Pakistan came to Dewsbury to work in the mills. However, after the oil crisis of 1973 the textile industry in Dewsbury began to collapse and the town has been in decline ever since.

If you were to float above the centre of Dewsbury on market day, you would see the life of the
town, its past and its present, laid bare. Signs of
the industrial age are everywhere: in the Methodist
churches and the grand looming arches of the town's
viaduct, in the old mills now converted into modern
'loft-style' apartments, in the handsome co-operative
buildings and the ornate clock tower of the town
hall. Meanwhile, on the streets below, the present
life of the town is on show as crowds of Asian families
weave through the market stalls. The Habibia shop
sells long gowns and headscarves; the mannequins
in the windows wear veils. Young white mothers
push prams quickly through the crowds as the rain
begins to fall. Asian mothers in headscarves gossip in
shop doorways.

I had arrived in the town on a late-autumn day
beneath darkening skies. The dullness of the day
added to the sullen atmosphere among the crowd of
reporters standing outside a house in an otherwise
quiet street in Thornhill Lees, a suburb of Dewsbury.
The close was made up of rows of neat, modern
two-up-two-down houses, many of them with narrow flowerbeds lining the concrete paths leading up
from the street. The communal lawns sloped down
to the pavement. The window panes of the front
doors were obscured by frosted glass or lace curtains

and yet there was also something very intimate about the houses in the close, squeezed together in this quiet, unremarkable suburb. In these late-Victorian terraced streets it would be hard to avoid your neighbours or miss the sounds of their domestic lives.

The photographers and reporters were on a 'watch', sent by their editors to sit and wait for a story. A watch can last for days or even weeks, if you're waiting for a court case to come to an end, or a politician to resign or a celebrity couple to emerge from hospital with a new baby. It means long cold days camped out with fellow reporters on streets like this one, occasionally engaging in chat, mostly staring into the road drinking endless cups of tea.

I found this watch particularly disturbing. We were waiting for Aisha Azmi to come out of her house. Azmi is a young British Muslim who was a teaching assistant at the local school. She had taken legal action against the school because she had been forbidden to wear the *niqab*, the full veil that covers the face except for the eyes, in class. When she had applied for the job of teaching assistant she had been wearing a headscarf only but later made the decision to attend lessons wearing the full veil. The school decided to ask her to remove it after complaints from pupils that they could not understand what she was saying. Azmi said she could remove the veil only if

there was no male member of staff present. This was
a condition that her employer, Kirklees Council,
could not agree to. The council suspended her on
full pay pending the outcome of the employment
tribunal. Her lawyers argued that she had been
discriminated against on religious grounds. The
court ruled that she had not been discriminated
against because of her religion but that she had
been victimized, and she was awarded compensation
of £1,100. Throughout the process every party
behaved sensitively, discreetly and fairly. Together,
Kirklees Council, Aisha Azmi, her family and the
lawyers seemed to me to reflect the 'British values'
that politicians and commentators so often feel are
under threat.

This story would not have resulted in such press
attention – it might have made the newspapers for a
couple of days and then disappeared – if it had not
been for an article Jack Straw, MP for Blackburn,
in neighbouring Lancashire, had written for the
Lancashire Evening Telegraph a few weeks earlier. In
it Mr Straw described meeting one of his constituents at his surgery. A couple had come to seek his
advice. The woman seemed to be the one doing the
talking. She was wearing the *niqab*. 'It was not the
first time I had conducted an interview with someone in a full veil, but this particular encounter,

though very polite and respectful on both sides, got me thinking. In part, this was because of the apparent incongruity between the signals which indicate common bonds – the entirely English accent, the couples' education (wholly in the UK) – and the fact of the veil. Above all, it was because I felt uncomfortable about talking to someone "face to face" whom I could not see.'

Jack Straw has represented tens of thousands of British Asian Muslims in Blackburn. As he admitted himself in the article, he had assisted fully veiled constituents before, so why had he suddenly become 'uncomfortable' about it and why had he felt the need to describe his discomfort in the local newspaper? He goes on: 'I decided that I wouldn't just sit there the next time a lady turned up to see me in a full veil, and I haven't . . . I explain that this is a country built on freedoms. As for the full veil, wearing it breaks no laws.' His argument seems to contradict itself: Mr Straw wants women to feel they are able to do what they want because 'this is a country built on freedoms' and yet he does not want them *to want* to wear an Islamic headscarf. 'I go on to say that I think, however, that the conversation would be of greater value if the lady took the covering from her face.' Would the woman, who had sought the advice of a politician, a man who holds authority and power in the country in which she lives, feel the conversation to have 'greater value' when she is asked, by that politician, to remove the clothing that represents her beliefs and traditions? The very act of going to see a politician demonstrates that the woman is both politically aware (she knows who her MP is, seeks him out and clearly values his position) and self-confident (she feels able to address one of the best-known politicians in this country in a 'face-to-face' conversation). The fact that she, rather than her husband, was the one addressing Mr Straw also says something about her status within her marriage. Mr Straw, however, is more preoccupied by her attire than her actions as it is what she is wearing that seems to hinder 'relations' between them. 'Would she, however, think hard about what I said – in particular about my concern that wearing the full veil was bound to make better, positive relations between the two communities more difficult? It was such a visible statement of separation and of difference. I thought a lot about raising this matter a year ago, and still more about writing this. But if not me, who?'

Soon this article became headline news across the nation's media. For several days the papers were once again filled with anecdotes confirming Jack Straw's suspicions that British Muslims were separating themselves from the rest of British society. Within the same week, many of Jack Straw's senior New Labour colleagues reiterated his views: Harriet Harman, Tessa Jowell, Peter Hain, Ruth Kelly, Gordon Brown joined the chorus. Twelve days after Jack Straw's article appeared, the Prime Minister weighed in. It was time for his regular press conference at No. 10. A reporter asked him if he felt a Muslim woman wearing a veil could make a contribution to British society. Tony Blair paused. His voice shifted, as if he was thinking about this question for the first time (hardly likely given the media attention the matter had received over the previous two weeks). 'That's a very difficult question,' he said. 'It is a mark of separation and that is why it makes other people from outside the community feel uncomfortable.'

No one seemed to have noticed that the woman who had worn this 'mark of separation' and thereby caused such grave concern among the press and political establishment was directly engaging in the democratic political process in this country.* She

*In the chapter entitled 'Hidden Lives' I explain how many young men see political engagement as the way to empower immigrant communities, offering hope and a part to play in British society – the very thing that this young woman seems to be trying to do.

was a member of the electorate and had gone to see her MP. This is something that few of us ever do, and it seems more significant to me than what she was wearing or the religion she practises. However, thanks in part to Tony Blair's statement and the supporting response from many of his colleagues in the Cabinet, the argument over the veil remained, and remains, an obsession for many and was the reason why people were camped outside the house of a young teaching assistant in a street in a Yorkshire town. Once again Tony Blair had weighed in on the issue, ignoring the usual legal restrictions and commenting directly on the case by saying that he backed the school's decision to suspend Azmi.

Standing in Azmi's street with a crowd of reporters on a cold, dank day in October I was reminded of my experience of a year before as I waited for the arrival of Ayaan Hersi Ali at the ICA. I was asking myself the same questions I had asked then: how did this story become so important? Why were people so exercised about it? What was I doing here? Debate seemed to have been reduced to hysteria. The point appeared to have been missed. Again, the establishment seemed to be reinforcing divide rather than seeking to reduce it. The veil had obscured issues of much greater importance. As we stood outside the house, a photographer told me that a picture of Azmi without her veil would fetch the lucky photographer £50,000. The reason for this particular watch became very clear.

The people of Dewsbury, both Muslim and non-Muslim, unfortunately have more serious things to worry about than the attire of their inhabitants. The town is in crisis. Ravensthorpe (a Muslim area) and Chickenley (originally home to the mining community and predominantly white) are among the 10 per cent most deprived areas in the UK. The unemployment rate in Dewsbury is around 40 per cent. The steady economic decline since the 1970s has led to greater social polarization and political tension between the Muslim and white communities; in 1989 Dewsbury experienced some of the worst race riots seen in Britain. Mohammed Siddique Khan, the ringleader of the 7th July bombers, moved to Dewsbury with his wife and young daughter in early 2005. They settled in Thornhill Lees, the suburb where Aisha Azmi lives. In 2006 the BNP won a seat on the local council.

Savile Town is home to many of Dewsbury's Asian Muslims. It feels like a ghetto. Even in very poor immigrant areas such as Tower Hamlets in London or Tiger Bay in Cardiff, home to a large population of Somalis, there are small shops, locally owned businesses and the pulse of life on the streets.

Savile Town, however, feels abandoned. It is hard to believe it is only nine miles from Leeds. The neighbourhood of Victorian redbrick terraces, first built to house mill workers, is edged by derelict wasteland. Among the houses stands Markazi Mosque, where Mohammed Siddique Khan used to worship.

After leaving Azmi's house behind I went to the mosque, just as Friday noon prayers were coming to an end. I approached some of the older men as they were leaving the building. They were polite but wary and very reluctant to talk to me. I asked if we could take a few shots of the streets around the mosque. They shrugged and walked away. As we started filming, one of the younger men ran over to us, shouting: 'Hey, stop filming! Stop filming, please.' He pulled his skullcap from his head and his voice grew angry: 'Put the camera down. Put it down.' He raised his arm to block the lens. 'It's people like you that give us a bad name. Get out of here! Get the fuck out!' More youths ran over to us and the crowd grew. Then a young man came forward. He was wearing jeans and no cap but a *keffiyah* (the traditional headdress worn in the Middle East; in this case a symbol of Palestinian nationalism). He looked to be in his late twenties, while the others appeared younger, in their late teens. He seemed to command respect from the crowd. He asked us where we were from and we explained that we were reporting for Al Jazeera. He tested our Arabic. The crowd seemed to give a collective sigh of relief. I heard one young man remark in a thick Yorkshire accent, 'Fuckin' 'ell, they're speaking a foreign language. Why can't they speak fuckin' English?' I caught the eye of a boy who was staring at me and smiling. 'Hey, Rageh, give us a wave!' he said.

The tension began to dissolve and the youths spoke more freely, but only on condition that our camera was turned off. Everyone in Savile Town was afraid to talk publicly about Islamic militancy or about Mohammed Siddique Khan's connection to the local mosque. The young man in the *keffiyah* explained, 'You'll get locked up if you talk about these things. That's what people think. If you mention them, you'll be associated with it. That's why no one wants to talk to the media.' He added that even the clerics would no longer speak. He had known Khan for the few months that he had worshipped at the mosque: 'He just seemed like any other religious, quiet young man. Why should we know he would do this when the school where he taught had no idea about him either?' After 7th July his own house had been raided and he had been arrested.

I asked the men what they thought about Jack Straw's comments on the veil. I had hardly finished my question when a ripple of laughter spread through the crowd. The young man spoke again: 'Nobody here minds talking about this at all. Let's have a debate, sure. But let's talk about some more important things first, like the chronic poverty in Dewsbury, the fact that a third of the people are unemployed, and that there's a drugs crisis.'

The drugs problem was the preoccupation of everyone I spoke to in Dewsbury, from the men outside the mosque to Farhana Haq, a young female journalist on the local *Batley News*. We had met earlier that day in the office of the newspaper, with its familiar feel: paper everywhere, empty coffee cups littering the desks. Farhana, a smiling woman in her early twenties, a headscarf framing her face, stood up to greet me. She was one of the local paper's three female reporters and the only Muslim. Reporting on local news had been tough for her at first: 'Being a Muslim and a journalist, local Muslims were suspicious of me in the beginning – thinking I was a sell-out or something. But then, when they saw my reports and saw that I could be fair and honest about my community and be a reporter at the same time, many young people were quite proud and some of them wanted to know how to get a job like mine.'

She too was very worried about drugs: 'The majority of the people who are in court are young Muslims. They're up for drugs: dealing and possession.'

For conservative Muslim families in economically deprived areas like Dewsbury, having a young relative associated with drug addiction or dealing is deeply shameful. There are also strong cultural forces that lead many families to keep the problem quiet and not seek help from outside, say through social services. Often the only people who can reach these troubled families are Islamist organizations. One such that has been very active in Savile Town is Hizb ut-Tahrir, an Islamist political party, banned in some countries, whose aim is to unite all Muslims in a single pan-Islamic state. Farhana explains: 'The organization seeks to help young men come off drugs as part of a social, religious and political process, a kind of Muslim reawakening which, for want of a better phrase, is like becoming a "reborn" Muslim. Faced with a relative who is addicted to drugs, many conservative Muslims are grateful to these organizations for helping.' Some of the organizations working on the drugs crisis in Savile Town are fundamentalist, some are benign, but all of them are offering help in a field of desperate need and to a community that feels increasingly unable to seek help from the wider world. The more marginalized and maligned by the establishment this community is, the more it will turn inwards, reaching for possibly extreme forms of salvation.

When I asked Farhana what she thought about the government and media obsession with the veil, she responded in similar ways to the young man outside the mosque. She was more concerned about the poverty in the area, the youths in court. She said that shortly after Jack Straw's article, as the voices of mainstream opinion critical of the veil grew ever louder, she noticed increasing numbers of young British Muslim women in Batley and Dewsbury wearing the veil. As she said: 'The veil is now our symbol of solidarity.'

The veil is not seen as political by those who do not wear it, but it is seen as deeply political by many of those women who do. It seems to run counter to the modern idea of individual identity and yet, for many Muslim women in a seemingly anti-Muslim age, it is a way of reclaiming an identity and a means of allying yourself with a group of people who feel either abandoned or under siege. But either way it distracts us from what matters. It distracts us from the fact that a young British Muslim woman in a veil looks to her local MP for help and advice; that a young, educated British Muslim woman is working in education in her local school; or that a young Muslim woman is a successful reporter on a newspaper in a Yorkshire town. It distracts us from the horrifying poverty of many immigrant communities in Britain; it distracts us from the plight of women in Afghanistan who are unable to go to school because of a war raging there, despite the fact that one of the British government's declared aims in their invasion of that country was to liberate its women; it distracts us from the news that on 6 October 2006, the day after Jack Straw's article appeared, a Muslim woman reported that her headscarf was ripped off and she was thrown to the ground by a white man at a London Underground station. *These* are the issues that matter and, whether women wear veils or not, these will continue to be the issues that define our society.

Postscript

It is almost a year since I recorded the many voices and stories in this book: the noisy chatter of Somali and white schoolgirls tumbling down the double-decker bus in Hounslow, Samia and her memories of flight from Hargeisa during the war. During this year I have, at times, felt pessimistic about the future for Muslims in this country. At the beginning of the book I quoted a friend, Jason Burke, and his response to US analysis directly after 9/11: 'There was a genuine interest in understanding "why". *Why* "they" hate us, *why* "they" were prepared to kill themselves, *why* such a thing could happen . . . That curiosity,' he wrote, 'has dwindled and is being replaced by other questions: *how* did it happen, *how many* of "them" are there, *how many* are there left to capture and kill?' I thought back then that things would begin to right themselves, that there would soon be a renewed desire to find some common ground between Muslims and non-Muslims in Britain. But this has not happened. Coverage of the issues continues to focus on what divides us rather than what unites us, whether it is in the way we criticize what Muslim women wear or when the Prime Minister declares that 'Our pride in being home to many cultures is being used against us.'

However, in the summer of 2006 I attended an event in East London that made me begin to feel hopeful again. I had been invited to speak at a theatre in Forest Gate, the area where, two weeks earlier, the Metropolitan Police had raided the house of a Muslim family and arrested two Muslim brothers. In the course of the operation, they had shot one of the young men in the shoulder. The police believed they were storing chemicals in their house to make weapons, but the intelligence turned out to be wrong and the officers found nothing incriminating.

After the incident the local church in the borough, who had supported the family throughout, offered to host a press conference in the church hall. When I saw Mohammed Abdul Kahar and Abul Koyair walk into the press conference, with their shaved heads and long beards, even I assumed that they would hold radical views and would use this occasion not only to criticize the police but to express a fundamentalist vision. Instead, in faltering voices, the two young men talked simply of how they sought to provide for their families and said that all they wanted was an apology from the police. They appeared the very opposite of religious fire-brands.

When I headed to Forest Gate two weeks later I was nervous. Emotions were still raw: local people were angry about the police action and frightened of what might happen next. And yet, as soon as I walked into the theatre, my nerves disappeared. The audience was made up of white middle-class elderly women and young Somali girls in headscarves, of groups of young Asian men and white students; there was a Somali man with his three small children, an elderly North African woman with her young daughter. The room was packed, alive with loud chatter.

I gave a short talk and then took questions from the audience. A middle-aged white lady stood up. She explained that she had not come to make a political point about the incident, just to say one thing: 'I live on Lansdowne Road, not far from where the two young boys live. Now, the newspapers make out that I live in some sort of ghetto. I don't! Our street is very mixed, there are white people, Muslims, Hindus, you name it. It's a nice area and I've lived here for many years, as have my neighbours.' When I asked her if she had felt more frightened or wary of her Muslim neighbours since the raid, she replied: 'Of course not. The only thing I'm frightened of is whether the police are going to knock down my door and shoot me in the middle of the night!' The audience laughed and people clapped.

This is, of course, only one person's experience, but I believe that it reflects the opinions of a much wider group of people who are not willing to presume the worst about their neighbours and fellow Britons, who do not wish to implicate a whole community in the murderous and hateful actions of a few individuals.

At times it has seemed impossible to change the minds of the establishment, to convince them that not all Muslims are terrorists, to explain to politicians that, if you condemn a group of people for separating themselves from mainstream society, they will only retreat further from that society. But it is essential that we do not despair for, at its heart, this message of division and fear is utterly without hope. It cannot and does not speak for the girls on the bus in Hounslow, or the journalist in Batley, or the travel agent in Ealing or for me. This pessimistic vision of a divided society, of people wishing to separate themselves from each other, whether it be Muslims from non-Muslims or the other way round, offers us nothing for the future of this country. That is why it has to fail.